# Easter Sermons

# Easter Sermons

From the Untrained Mind

Robert Tippett

Copyright © 2020

All rights reserved. Produced in the United States of America. No part of this publication may be reproduced, or transmitted, in any form or by any means electronic, mechanical, photocopying, recording, or otherwise, without the prior written permission of the author.

ISBN 978-1-952076-02-2 Paperback
ISBN 978-1-952076-03-9 Epub

Published by Katrina Pearls, LLC

# Dedication

This book is dedicated to the memory of my loving wife, who passed away in late 2019. Joycelyn Tippett was a fellow Apostle; my partner in service to God. She was the editor of my books and everything I have written since we married in 2006. She is greatly missed by a world that needs more like her. I am comforted by her continued spiritual presence with me and the insight to this series of books I owe to that presence.

# Table of Contents

Dedication .................................................... 5
From the Untrained Mind ....................... 9
A Season Named Easter ......................... 21

## Year A
Easter Sunday ......................................... 45
Second Sunday of Easter ..................... 55
Third Sunday of Easterr ...................... 67
Fourth Sunday of Easter ..................... 79
Fifth Sunday of Easter ......................... 91
Sixth Sunday of Easter ........................ 99
Seventh Sunday of Easter .................. 111
Pentecost Sunday ................................. 121

## Year B
Easter Sunday ......................................... 135
Second Sunday of Easter ..................... 149
Third Sunday of Easter ....................... 159
Fourth Sunday of Easter ..................... 173
Fifth Sunday of Easter ......................... 189
Sixth Sunday of Easter ........................ 203
Seventh Sunday of Easter .................. 215
Pentecost Sunday ................................. 231

## Year C

| | |
|---|---|
| Easter Sunday | 247 |
| Second Sunday of Easter | 263 |
| Third Sunday of Easter | 275 |
| Fourth Sunday of Easter | 287 |
| Fifth Sunday of Easter | 301 |
| Sixth Sunday of Easter | 315 |
| Seventh Sunday of Easter | 327 |
| Pentecost Sunday | 341 |

# From the Untrained Mind

The sermons contained in this book are a collection of those offered up on my Wordpress blog, entitled "Bus Stop Sermons." The Easter sermons (including Pentecost Sunday sermons) total twenty-four that have been collected from over one hundred seventy posts there. I have written all of the posts. The totality of those posts cover every Sunday over a three-year span of time, with the motivation being the schedule of readings from the Holy Bible, as posted by the Episcopal Church's Lectionary. Included in that schedule are the eight Sundays in the season of Easter, with the last Sunday in that season being both the end of Easter and the beginning of the Ordinary Season numbered as "After Pentecost." Since the Episcopal Lectionary cycle takes three years before recycling (Years A, B, and C), eight times three equals twenty-four.

The disclaimer that must be understood is this: None of the words presented here (or any of those still there on Wordpress) have ever been spoken out loud before an audience of any kind. In that sense, they are imaginary orations.

My imagination stems from the movie *Forrest Gump* and the scenes where Forrest would be seen at a bus stop telling his life story to strangers. I imagine doing the same,

Easter Sermons: From the Untrained Mind

only differently. I see my captive audience as one that is not forced to sit and wait for a bus to come take them some place they desire to be. Instead, they are seeking the goal of heaven, or at least some insight into Christian lessons. Christianity can be seen like a transit system that parallels public transportation.

Those who read my words will then be much like the ones Forrest talked with: patiently bored; interested while waiting, but getting to one's destination on a planned schedule being more important; embarrassed by the thought that an imbecile has anything worthwhile to offer; outright rejection with ridicule; or willing recipients of an engaging story. Over the past five years many people have visited at my bus stop. Several have actually liked what they read and a few have felt something I wrote demanded that they make a comment.

Like what Forrest shared at his bus stop, everything I offer is designed as a friendly exchange with strangers. It is my story, not the story of anyone else. The commonality of the lectionary readings and how they make me remember my life story makes me share what I saw, what I felt, and what I think needs to happen for me to get on that bus to heaven. After all, everyone going to a bus stop is there for the same purpose, even if the ends of their rides differ.

As I am waiting like everyone else, I remember my life with words, based on images passing before my mind's eye. The reality of my memories being expressed can seem like I am looking at someone sitting right next to me on the bus stop bench, talking to him or her. My memories of my life can become so vivid that it seems like I am telling others what to do, when that is not the case at all. I have become God, through the Mind of Christ, telling myself what God wants me to do. It is like preaching to the choir, when preacher and choir are all the same person – a one man band form of church.

The history that had me write imaginary sermons is based on my relationship with my wife. My wife would become an Episcopal priest, but before she made that transformation she was a church-lady Episcopalian. She was raised in that religious denomination as a girl and had a renewed commitment, as to the depth of her involvement with that branch of Christianity, before we met. Thus, I found myself becoming acquainted with that form of religious worship.

I had been unchurched for roughly forty years, prior to being introduced to Episcopalianism. In that time I had not been heathen, in regards to belief in God and Jesus Christ. I had become disenchanted with organized religion at the age of sixteen and repulsed completely by my mid-twenties, due to the televangelism that so blatantly besmirched Christianity as a form of entertainment, with actors crying crocodile tears while they begged for money, promising ministries that offered Jesus theme parks to their paying fans. My first wife was raised a Methodist, and I set aside my dislike for churches on Christmas and Easter and whenever the nearby church offered reasonably priced softball leagues.

For as little as my church involvement had been, I never stopped feeling that I could talk with God at any time. My childhood religious upbringing had instilled a sense of closeness to God that made prayer be informal and constant. For as wayward as my life would roam, I always felt that God was with me, watching out for me. I never attempted to shame anyone for their religious beliefs or commitments to organized religion; but I rarely felt a need to go to a church, even though I often begged God for His forgiveness after feeling the guilt of sin.

My life changed completely in 2001. I began wandering down the path God had always planned for me to walk, knowing that I would wander the path I had taken to get to that point. Everything in my life began to be seen clearly as purposeful and necessary, grooming me for the road ahead. I suddenly was given an ability to understand the writings of Nostradamus, even though what I was shown was just the grand scope of view. It would take me another seven years to reach the microscope level of detailed awareness.

It was during that time of my life that I began writing books that attempted to explain Nostradamus to the world. It was during that time of my life that I met the woman who would become my second wife. It was during that time of my life that I began regular attendance in Episcopalian churches.

God brought my wife and I together, for the purpose of walking our chosen paths that led to God. My wife had ideas of serving the Episcopalian Church as a priest. I had ideas about telling the world about Nostradamus being an Apostle of Jesus Christ. Once God joined our paths together, my wife had a plan to serve God as an ordained priest (Episcopalian schooled and metaphysically educated) and I had a plan to serve God as an unordained priest (metaphysically schooled and divinely educated). My wife and I, together, became like two sides of the same coin, as two souls with the same purpose, from different perspectives.

Sunday after Sunday my wife and I sat in a pew and listened to one lame sermon after another. As I read the handout bulletin that had the Scriptural readings printed on them, I was reading them with an ability to understand, based on the similarity of writing style I found in Scripture and that by Nostradamus. By being able to make sense of Nostradamus, the meanings of the Scripture readings became obvious to me. However, as obvious as it was to me, that clarity was not being expressed in pulpit oratory.

Each Sunday my wife and I would discuss this absence of explanation in church. My wife agreed with me. She confessed that she had never known so much was contained in the verses read aloud, as she had never placed great interest in reading the Holy Bible. The more we discussed these matters, the deeper our faith in God became. My wife wanted to fulfill an absence in the Episcopal Church with divine insight and holy knowledge. I wanted to tell the world that every book of the Holy Bible had been written by servants of God, just as Nostradamus had written a most holy book that was unrecognized as such.

My wife and I began a ministry of learning, where we attended bible study classes, lectionary classes, and began visiting a variety of Episcopal churches to listen to a variety of priests giving sermons. We found that the education of Episcopal priests did not allow them to see or promote the meaning that was found hidden in the Holy Scriptures, lingering at the origin language level, while demanding divine assistance in discerning the truth. Instead of the accepting my offerings (while my wife patiently observed and listened), my observations were often rejected outright, questioned as to where I had read such things, and tossed out like dirty bath water when I admitted I had no pedigree, such as a degree from a divinity school.

This was the same rejection I faced when telling others that Nostradamus was misunderstood, due to a mistaken desire to read divine syntax as paraphrased English. My wife, always the smarter of the two of us, saw that being able to attend seminary was dependent on not rocking the boat (or nave). She realized it would be impossible for her to serve God as an Episcopal priest, if the Episcopal Church banned her from seminary school. So, she was discerned, approved, and selected for official education (she already possessed a PhD from academia), meaning my wife was further down the path from church-lady to ordained priest. Meanwhile, I continued to focus on writing books about Nostradamus, leaving my religious interpretations for another time. Then, it was off to seminary together, my wife the student and me the spouse.

While in seminary, my wife and I lived in an enchanted land that was reminiscent of Disney World. Everywhere we turned there was someone in costume, with the whole campus like a movie set. Visiting for a week allows one to be mesmerized by the pretence, but living there and working there brought about an ugly sense of reality. The seminarians there proved, more often than not, to be reborn college drinking buddies and frat house pranksters. There were few who wanted to talk about their core faith after classes were over.

As a way to make three years pass by without screaming, "No! This can't be!" I wrote and self-published four books that explained Nostradamus and his prophecies. My busy work allowed my wife the luxury of not being distracted by my negativity.

In May 2013, my wife graduated from seminary and was soon after ordained as a deacon for the Episcopal Church, Diocese of Mississippi. She interviewed and was offered a medium-sized town's parish, which she gladly accepted. In the month before her official start, I began to write sermons that were based on the Episcopal Lectionary, from which my wife's sermons would be based. I determined that I would maintain this program for an entire three-year cycle. I not only had written a sermon for the first Sunday that my wife would officially begin ministering to her new flock, but I also had several sermons written for the following several Sundays.

I wrote those sermons for myself, but also as discussion material between me and my wife. My wife read every one of my sermons over that three-year cycle (completed in about 32 months). She occasionally used a snippet or a paraphrase from something I had written, never referencing me directly (per my request), in her own prepared sermons (the official ones). Because my sermons were written about my life, which is highly unique (as everyone's life is), they can only be presented by me. Still, my words had an influence on my wife, just as her words influenced me.

I originally posted my sermons on a GoDaddy website, but the expense to maintain it did not match the results. When I ended the idea of having a website for both Nostradamus and Christian writings (separately grouped), I created free Wordpress blogs and reposted them there. When the idea of a blog named "Bus Stop Sermons" came to be, I subtitled that name with "From the Untrained Mind."

## Easter Sermons: From the Untrained Mind

That subtitle is also placed on this book, with the reasoning being that I have no diploma that gives me an official pulpit, no official approval to lead a flock of followers, and no vast educational history of study that proves me intellectually adept at sermon writing. But, then, I don't believe Jesus, nor the first many waves of true Christian Apostles and Saints had sheepskins from the University of the Holy Spirit.

The subtitle should be obvious, because everything on my "Bus Stop Sermons" blog and everything from there republished here comes from one who has no training in preaching sermons. My wife, and all officially ordained priests, are "trained" to preach and also "trained" to follow ritual dogma and employer protocol. That education, more than giving theology students the secrets to obtaining the hidden meaning that Holy Scripture contains, "trains" them to do a sermon that is close to being only twelve minutes in length.

As I was rereading the sermons that I presented for Easter, it seems I also tried to keep away from any depth of explanation. By staying on a path that was based on my life and how the readings played out in my life's likes and experiences, I doubt anyone would walk out on me, if I were ordained and had a congregation to which I would preach my messages.

I once had a fellow parishioner confide to me that he became an Episcopalian simply because of the short sermons. He had been a member of a more 'southern' denomination, which had a preacher routinely present two hour sermons, with everyone expected to stay after church, to eat and get to know one another more. My wife also had to conform to those constraints; but like me, she had to prepare her sermons and print them out so she would not go off track and take too long. If I were to ad lib one of my sermons, I imagine I could wander for a couple of hours easy.

When I say "mind," I do that to differentiate the source of my knowledge. It is not from a brain that has studies the Holy Bible for decades. Like my wife had spent little time in her early history reading Scripture, I too was very Biblical illiterate. I knew the basic Bible Stories, but there was so much that the lectionary exposed me to that I barely recognized. When I took a course designed to educate laypersons for ministry, I was in a class of Episcopalians who knew just as little. However, I was better prepared from having studied before going to classes, and often from having written about what the course focused on each week, than were the other students in the class.

The point of an "untrained mind" is not to be a statement about how full of wisdom I am or how deeply I have read books about the meaning of Scripture, without ever getting a diploma (or even a gold star on a report), because there are not many people (if any) that see Scripture like I see it. Just as when I was learning to read the divine language that is ever-present in the writings of Nostradamus, there was no human being who was teaching a course in how to do that. The "untrained mind" is then metaphor for an openness to receive the Spirit of knowledge and speak the truth. While the brain functions in this process, it is not the organ originating higher thoughts. It simply receives them and then I have to figure the meaning by following impulses of insight.

As a twist of irony, I was raised in an Assembly of God church. That church is known for being in the "Pentecostal" branch of Christian denominations. The name "Pentecostal" is based on the Day of Pentecost, when disciples suddenly began "speaking in tongues." Many times I witnessed people (one woman more than others) stand up in church and begin making sudden, loud, unintelligible repetitive noises, with hands raised high. For some reason, Pentecostals believe making such noises constitutes being filled with the Holy Spirit. As I was sixteen when I voluntarily left that denomination, and had received some "training" in how to become tongue-tied and appear to be "speaking in tongues," I never believed making throat noises served any purpose; but then I was too young and ignorant to really know what was going on in church at that age.

Many years later, while in a church Bible study class, a young man said the unintelligible noises have to then be interpreted by someone who is fluent in "speaking in tongues." Supposedly, after a public display of noise making, someone then stands up and explains, "She said (this or that)." In all my youthful years of attending an Assembly of God church, where regularly the same woman would put on her display, I never heard anyone stand up and explain what she had said. All I heard were whispered "Praise the Lords" and then the pastor would continue where he left off. As such, I can assure everyone that "speaking in tongues" has absolutely nothing to do with making unintelligible noises.

What I do is the reality of "speaking in tongues," where the Greek word "*glōssais*" is translated as "tongues," but also can say "languages." Acts 2 sets up how pilgrims (Jews and Israelites) from many different places marvelled at how the Apostles suddenly began "speaking in other languages" (from the Greek *"lalein heterais glōssais"*), due to the Holy Spirit making them speak in the tongues of others. Understanding Nostradamus meant the Holy Spirit made me see the text of Nostradamus (the literal Old French, not the English paraphrases) and be led to see how vast the meaning was. Learning how to read in that divine "tongue" (via the Holy Spirit, as it must be with me to see the truth) means I interpret that which was spoken in tongues. Like the young man said, I prove that to be true. People read Holy Scripture and sit silently, not knowing what has been said (although some whisper "Praise the Lord"). I stand up to interpret what was stated.

I share this history not to make myself seem special. Anyone who devotes him or herself to God and sincerely prays for His guidance, can likewise do what I do. Just remember what I said about seeing only the grand scope when I first started understanding Nostradamus. It took years of dedication and devotion to follow the whispers of insight and see the depth of truth that would be revealed through divine texts.

It then becomes a test at the bus stop. Like the one woman that told Forrest, after he said, "Isn't that your bus?" She just waved her hand and said, "There will be another one." She wanted to hear more about what Forrest had to say.

That is what a good sermon does. It lights a fire of interest. It burns within one's heart so they cannot ignore the call to "Look deeper" anymore. I pray these sermons will ignite others to be filled with the Holy Spirit and preach their own bus stop sermons.

Easter Sermons: From the Untrained Mind

# A Season Named Easter

Easter is undoubtedly the most revered day of recognition for all who profess to be Christians. Easter is the day our lord and savior rose from death; belief in that rising is what separates Christians from Jews and all other religions. Thus, Easter Sunday is the one day in the liturgical year that demands attendance, above all other days.

When I was an unchurched adult, married to my first wife (who had been raised in a Methodist church but had also willfully become unchurched as a married woman), the few times that I remember wearing a suit and tie and going to a local Methodist church was Easter Sunday. I do not have vivid memories of having gone to a Methodist church for Christmas, but Christmas is the second most important time for a Christian to go to church. That reason is belief in Jesus as one's Savior, which demands recognition as to when God sent His Son into the world to save us. However, there are differences between Easter and Christmas that should be understood.

First of all, Christmas reflects a Christian's praise to Jesus for having been born into the world to save his followers. Easter is then the second birth of Jesus, which Christians also praise greatly. This means Jesus has two birthdays each year: one when a newborn baby; and, one when a reborn adult. At both times of birth, Christians recognize that Jesus was the Promised Savior, as the Messiah or the Christ. However, knowing that the life of a born baby Jesus and the life of a reborn adult Jesus is followed by a swift departure from the public eye, it is difficult for many Christians to grasp why birth and rebirth are so important in their personal lives.

Second, Easter is always on a Sunday, but Christmas only occasionally falls on a Sunday. Over the past ten years (2010 to 2019), Christmas fell on a Sunday in 2011 and 2016, which was twice in five years. Christmas will next fall on a Sunday in 2022, where a six-year period will have passed since the last Sunday Christmas. A Christmas service at church (usually a nighttime event, if not a midnight mass) is so often held on a week day that the Sunday following the December 25th day marks the beginning of the "Christmas Season," or the Twelve Days of Christmas that begin on Christmas Day. Those years when Christmas actually falls on a Sunday often means a midnight mass celebration, with the normal church hours for a Sunday service suspended.

This brings up the third difference. Everyone knows when to expect Christmas to come. It is a birthdate fixed in Christian mindsets. December 25th is seen as the birthday of Jesus, born in a stable and then placed into manger in Bethlehem. Although that date is arbitrarily set, with many seeing how the Roman Church affixed the birth of our Christ to pagan rituals that observed the Winter Solstice, Christians know when to expect a "birthday party." Easter, on the other hand, is one of those dates that require someone (a church calendar or the Internet) to tell Christians when Easter will be recognized, as the date changes from year to year. While many Christians realize these fluctuations are due to when the Jewish Passover is, most do not understand why the Passover changes from year to year, effecting when Easter is recognized.

Not only do Rome and all the Protestant denominations of Western Christianity usually celebrate Easter at different times than the Jews recognize Passover, the Eastern Orthodox Church is more closely aligned with the Jewish recognition than that determined by Rome. Here is a list that shows how hard it is for a typical Christian to know when Easter will be recognized.

| Year | Western (Both) Easter | Orthodox Easter | Jewish Passover | Last Day (of the week) |
|---|---|---|---|---|
| 2010 | (April 4) | | March 30 – April 6 | (Tuesday) |
| 2011 | (April 24) | | April 19 – April 26 | (Tuesday) |
| 2012 | April 8 | April 15 | April 7 – April 14 | (Saturday) |
| 2013 | March 31 | May 5 | March 26 – April 2 | (Tuesday) |
| 2014 | (April 20) | | April 15 – April 22 | (Tuesday) |
| 2015 | April 5 | April 12 | April 4 – April 11 | (Saturday) |
| 2016 | March 27 | May 1 | April 23 – April 30 | (Saturday) |
| 2017 | (April 16) | | April 11 – April 18 | (Tuesday) |
| 2018 | April 1 | April 8 | March 31 – April 7 | (Saturday) |
| 2019 | April 21 | April 28 | April 20 – April 27 | (Saturday) |
| 2020 | April 12 | April 19 | April 9 – April 16 | (Thursday) |
| 2021 | April 4 | May 2 | March 28 – April 4 | (Sunday) |
| 2022 | April 17 | April 24 | April 16 – April 23 | (Saturday) |
| 2023 | April 9 | April 16 | April 6 – April 13 | (Thursday) |
| 2024 | March 31 | May 5 | April 23 – April 30 | (Tuesday) |
| 2025 | (April 20) | | April 13 – April 20 | (Sunday) |
| 2026 | April 5 | April 12 | April 2 – April 9 | (Thursday) |
| 2027 | March 28 | May 2 | April 22 – April 29 | (Thursday) |
| 2028 | (April 16) | | April 11 – April 18 | (Tuesday) |
| 2029 | April 1 | April 8 | March 31 – April 7 | (Saturday) |
| 2030 | April 21 | April 28 | April 18 – April 25 | (Thursday) |

Easter Sermons: A Season Named Easter

This chart[1] makes it clear that only six times out of a twenty-one year span do the Roman churches (Western) and Orthodox churches (Eastern) agree on when Easter Sunday should be recognized. In the other fifteen years, ten times they recognize two different Sundays a week apart. In those cases, the Roman churches always recognize Easter a week ahead of the Eastern churches. On five other years, the Roman churches recognize Easter Sunday in late March or early April, whereas the Orthodox churches wait until early May to do so. Meanwhile, the Jewish Passover will begin and end on a *Shabbat* (as did the Passover of Jesus' arrest, trial, execution and burial) seven years out of twenty-one. Each Sunday that follows that end of the Passover festival on a sabbath day is recognized by the Orthodox churches as Easter Sunday, which would be a correct interpretation of Jesus being found not in his tomb on the first day of the week (*yom rishon*). The Roman churches, however, always recognize a Sunday that falls within the Jewish Passover timeframe, not after.

This difference of opinion, determined by the leaders of Christian churches, brings up questions as to why does Easter have to be recognized only on Sunday, when Christmas is fixed to one date and is recognized on different days of the week. The answer is obviously connected to the Gospel stories that tell of the "first day of the week" (*yom rishon*) as when Jesus was discovered out of his tomb and then appeared to his followers at different times, in different forms. This question becomes the epicenter of the difference between Judaism and Christianity, where one group of believers in the One God recognize *Shabbat* (Saturday) as

[1] Compiled from two sources on the Internet: https://www.calendarpedia.com/when-is/orthodox-easter.html and https://www.infoplease.com/calendar-holidays/major-holidays/jewish-holidays.

holy, whereas the other recognizes Sunday (the first day of the week) as such. Easter has to be seen as why Christians go to church on Sunday.

The Easter Season, as a liturgical period during a calendar year, must be seen through this lens that divides fifty-two weeks into fifty-two Sundays. The determination of when Easter Sunday occurs then sets the whole of the church calendar (those who adhere to the Roman-Anglican-Western schedule). Whereas Christmas is a date fixed in a year, like the birth of belief in Jesus fixes Christians to Christianity, Easter Sunday becomes the marker for all the seasons that occur in the rebirth of Jesus Christ in Christians. Because all Christians are reborn as Jesus Christ, that re-birthday becomes affixed to a day of the week, rather than a day of the year. Christians then recognize Sunday as the first day of the week that Christ was born into them.

The problem with that marker is there are many Jews who believed that Jesus was the Christ (their promised Messiah) and they never saw reason to abandon the Sabbath (*Yom Shabbat* or Saturday) as the seventh day that was made holy by God. In addition, God's Covenant made it clear that the Sabbath was not Sunday, when it states: "Observe the Sabbath day ["*yom shabbat*"] by keeping it holy, as the LORD your God has commanded you." (Deuteronomy 5:12) When Jesus said, "Do not think that I have come to abolish the Law or the Prophets; I have not come to abolish them but to fulfill them," (Matthew 5:17) this should also apply to recognizing the Sabbath as Saturday, not Sunday.

In the same sense, Jesus took part in every commanded festival that God said should forever be observed. Relative to the Passover, where Jesus would be the Paschal Lamb, God said "This is a day you are to commemorate; for the generations to come you shall celebrate it as a festival to the LORD--a lasting ordinance." (Exodus 12:14) The determination of when the Passover festival must be remembered is stated as, "In the first month you are to eat bread made without yeast, from the evening of the fourteenth day until the evening of the twenty-first day." (Exodus 12:18) Therefore, Jesus never said to abandon this commitment made in service to Yahweh.

As the above chart shows, Christians do yearly observe recognition of the Passover, but they do so in a way that is different than the Jews, because of the acceptance of Jesus as the Christ. To see this observance requires a closer inspection of the liturgical calendar, as Christians do not observe the Festival of Unleavened Bread in the same way as do Jews. To see this, one needs to return to the Lenten schedule and see the common practices there that prepare one to see the Passover recognition (where all firstborn male children would be spared, if their home was protected by the blood of a lamb) in a different light.

The period of Lent is forty days long and is a season fixed as such. Lent ends on Palm Sunday, always the Sunday before Easter. While Lent begins with a remembrance of Jesus being tested in the wilderness, after having gone forty days without food, the mistake is to see the forty days as a historical equivalent of the life of Jesus.

Each Christian is asked to sacrifice of him or herself during the Lenten Season, which has never been intended to be seen as a New Year's resolution redo. The sacrifice of Lent is then parallel to having no yeast in one's household. Lent is not about Jesus being tested, but those who follow in the steps of Jesus to become themselves unleavened bread. Sacrifice of worldly delights (the yeast of the earth plane) makes one receive the marking of the blood of Christ, so one is spared from death.

It is common practice in Episcopal churches (as well as Roman Catholic churches and others of similar religious dogma) to recognize each Wednesday during Lent as a time to recite the "Stations of the Cross" devotion and prayers. This service is also called "the Way of Sorrows" or the "*Via Crucis.*" As Lent begins on Ash Wednesday, there are six evening when those who participate in this reenactment of Jesus at his cross of death are actually preparing themselves to be the sacrificial lamb that following Palm Sunday when the Passion play is recited. This makes Lent be the preparation for the Passover Lamb's blood to become that which will give rise to unleavened bread on Easter Sunday. However, before one can rise again, one must first die of self.

Lent prepares one to die of self, while Easter represents when Jesus has resurrected within a true Christian. The Passover recognized by the Jews has been replaced by the forty days of fasting from leavening. The readings of Palm Sunday remind Christians of the arrest, trials, tortures and death Jesus experienced, which should reflect the same sacrifices one of his true disciples has experienced in the willing surrender of one's own self-ego. The eight days of a Jewish Passover become as symbolic as the forty days of self-denial, both timeframes being metaphor for a lifetime of sin being surrendered for an eternity of true life with God.

The 'angel of death' is then the mortality of human life, which will pass over all souls (the first born) that occupy human flesh (a household). Those souls that will be saved from this 'death' are those that have the blood of Christ above their 'doorways," which means the Mind of Christ painted across their brains that so easily fall prey to the sins of the world. To have the Christ Mind leads one's mental and bodily actions, one must be a household that has been cleaned out of the leavening of mortal life; this is Lent equating to God's commandment to observe the Passover Festival.

Instead of a Christian Passover, all of the churches (east and west) observe "Holy Week." This constitutes a quasi-equivalent to Passover week. The Episcopal Church offers services each day during Holy Week (as do others), but the two days that stand out, having special names, are Maundy Thursday and Good Friday. These two days are cause for some confusion that needs to be explained.

The origin of the word "Maundy" is, according to Dictionary.com: "1250–1300; Middle English *maunde* < Old French *mande* < Latin *mandātum* command, mandate (from the opening phrase *novum mandātum* (Vulgate) of Jesus' words to the disciples after He had washed their feet)."

This Latin Vulgate source comes from John 13:34, which states (in Latin), "*mandatum novum do vobis ut diligatis invicem sicut dilexi vos ut et vos diligatis invicem.*" That translates to English as, "A new command I give you: Love one another. As I have loved you, so you must love one another." The Greek text states, "*Entolēn kainēn didōmi hymin hina agapate allēlous ; kathōs ēgapēsa hymas hina kai hymeis agapate ēgapēsa .*" The part of John's thirteenth chapter that tells of Jesus washing feet take up verses four through seventeen, which is well before this statement of "a new commandment" being given by Jesus.

As Jesus did wash the feet of his disciples, he did not do that on a Thursday. Jesus did not give a new commandment to wash feet. In addition, from my personal experience as the spouse of an Episcopal priest, Maundy Thursday is sparsely attended AND those who do attend (for the most part) abstain from taking their socks and shoes off and letting someone wash their feet (like Simon Peter), although some (not many) will come to wash the feet of others. This rejection by modern Christians, as a direct reflection of Simon-Peter having been reborn many times over, shows the period of self-sacrifice (the forty days of Lent) has done little to prepare Christians to check their self-egos at the door and stop thinking:

> "'I' will have none of this, as 'I' declare you are too important to stoop so low as to wash anyone's feet."

Keep in mind how well-prepared Simon-Peter was to accept the arrest of Jesus and the threat his big brain presumed would be cast upon him, should anyone recognize him as a follower of Jesus. In the same Seder meal evening, after Jesus washed the feet of his disciples, he told that one would betray him. Then, after he gave his disciples his "new commandment," Simon-Peter was so bold as to presume, "I will lay down my life for you," only to have Jesus tell him, "Before the cock crows, you will deny me three times."

Everyone who professes to be Christian should see him or herself as Simon-Peter; if the ego has not been so surrendered so that one will gladly wash the feet of others that are also true Christians, then one is just as much a blowhard as was Simon-Peter.

One has to be reduced to an obedient servant of God to even begin to heed any new commandments given, especially one that says, "Love one another. As I have loved you, so you must love one another." One cannot hear Jesus as the one giving a new commandment, but God the Father. For anyone who has even been a father (or a mother), who would not love washing the little feet and toes of their own baby? That then becomes a true reflection of the state of being one has been reduced to, if one is to be a child of God, to be reborn as His Son (many times over).

It is most important that this familial love that Jesus spoke of, as his "New Commandment," does not expand beyond the bounds of blood relationship. Just as God did not save the first born male children of Pharaoh or the other Egyptians, the love of the Father to the children of Israel was selective love. Jesus was not teaching his "Little children" (from the capitalized Greek word "*Teknia*," found beginning John 13:33) to love Muslim refugees or love atheists, Communists, and even the Romans and leaders of the Temple Jews, because those were enemies and neighbors that demanded a separate form of love. Those who took in the Passover Seder bread and wine were the ones Jesus' "New Covenant" was for alone.

It is not coincidence that Jesus gave that new law to those who remained after Judas had departed (John 13:30b), as Judas was no longer part of the family of the Father. In that sense, Jesus washed the feet of Judas, showing a willingness to serve the Father beyond family; but the "New Testament" says that **all** true Christians must love one another, which is the founding principle of a new Church. Rather than a statement about new temples being built in the future to house God, "love one another; as I have loved you" says each true Christians must support other true Christians, as all true Christians are servants of the same Father, reborn as the same Son, so others also can be called to become true Christians. Jesus commanded his followers to take care of the family of Christ, first and foremost.

In the readings of Palm Sunday, the events of this Last Seder preceded the week that Jesus would face, before he would be found guilty, with his body hanging dead on a cross for two days. The transition from Palm Sunday to Maundy Thursday and then Good Friday can (and does) confuse those who profess belief in Jesus as the Christ to think Jesus was arrested, tried, convicted, executed and hung on a cross all on Thursday. Then Good Friday was when someone said, "Enough!" and his body was taken down and prepared for burial. Again, the events of Holy Week are symbolic of the Passover Week and not to be read as historically correct.

Repeatedly, Jesus said, "The Son of Man is going to be betrayed into the hands of men. They will kill him, and after three days he will rise." (Matthew 17:23) The actual Greek written says "*trite hēmera*," which translates as "third day." When "third" (as an ordinal number) can be twisted as "parts of three," not necessarily "a full three," the translation of "*hēmera*" as "the period from sunrise to sunset" means "after a third period from sunrise to sunset" has passed. That means "three days dead."

When one does the simple math, Jesus was executed on Wednesday [think back to all the Wednesday lessons of Lent now] and by "day" Friday, after he had been dead almost two days, the body was taken down, prepared, and temporarily entombed until the Sabbath had passed. That Sabbath would be the "third day."

The term "Good Friday" is then misleading, as "good" implies something positive. This name has been questioned, with the most logical explanation being that "good" actually comes from "holy," or "*sanctus*." Jesus was not crucified on a Friday, as the Gospels say his body was requested (by Joseph of Arimathea) to be taken down for preparation on that day of the week ("the day of preparation" means "Friday").

It was also sold that Friday morning as a good thing for Pilate to do, seeing how so many pilgrims in Jerusalem thought Jesus was holy, and seeing dead Jews on crosses on the Sabbath (most especially holy ones) could be inflammatory. Therefore, it was a "good" day to prepare for the end of the Passover festival by removing crucified bodies from view, when pilgrims would be heading out of Jerusalem and going by Golgotha (on Sunday, after a festival-ending *Shabbat*).

It is also important to know that Pilate knew the rules for taking down crucified criminals, as that method of death was known to make death by suffocation last days. Lasting anguish was a built-in deterrent to crime; so it was a slow, excruciating method of death, with the moans and groans of the dying a public lesson for all future criminals to see and hear, hopefully causing them not to choose crime. It should be grasped that the festival was **the excuse** presented to Pilate, because so many foreigners made policing expressions of anger harder to manage.

Robert Tippett

The request to take down crucified Jews on Friday morning also included the two beside Jesus. Because they showed signs of life still being in them, their leg bones were shattered by sledge hammers, causing them to collapse so their breathing completely was impeded. Jesus, on the other hand, showed no signs of life, so his side was pierced by a spear and his bodily fluids flowed down; so his legs were not broken by his showing no signed of nerve response. We are told that fulfilled prophecy. (John 19:36 – "These things happened so that the scripture would be fulfilled: "Not one of his bones will be broken.")

Remembering how Palm Sunday was a lengthy ceremony that recalled the Passion of the Christ, Christians must see that the trials, whipping, purple robing, crown of thorns, and crucifixion of Jesus was spread over a Passover festival period of eight days, which began on a Friday evening. That then led to a Wednesday darkening of the sun, earthquake, and curtain in the Temple being torn from top to bottom (at 3:00 PM). Jesus being taken down on Friday says a week had passed. We remembered that timing at the end of Lent. Thus, the rehashing of the foot washing event and the timing of Jesus being taken down from the cross, as Church ceremony during "Holy" Week, means "Good" Friday is little more than the Friday before Easter is recognized.

Because the Church (several denominations) does not recreate a chronology of Jesus' life, but creates metaphor for individual sacrifices and ego-deaths, "Holy Week" becomes just a way to wait out the death of Jesus before he can be resurrected on a Christian Sunday. Palm Sunday left everyone hanging on the cross with Jesus, without telling us to realize that was Wednesday. The lack of real time being shown makes it difficult to grasp "three days dead" over a week's time (from Sunday to Sunday). Holy Week is therefore just an intermission, before the most important day in all true Christians takes place (and that becomes an extension of Lent, more than a precursor of Easter).

Perhaps the worst name for a day in Holy Week is "Holy Saturday," which is not known for packing in the Christians for a Eucharistic event. Rather than see Saturday as the true Sabbath, regardless of whether or not Christians observe Saturday (*yom shabbat*) as their holy day, it remains forever the day Yahweh said observe it as holy. Instead of churches honoring that commitment (it was the Israelites and Jews, not us!), the Saturday before Easter Sunday is known for magical appearances of the Easter bunny, who always leaves lots of real and candy eggs for children to hunt on that holy day. This, of course, is the pagan link to Easter as a rite of spring and the fertility of the land and people and the renewal of growth to the earth.

Another aspect of the Easter Season is that is extends beyond Easter Sunday seven weeks. The reasoning for that number of Sundays is the math: seven (weeks) times seven (days per week) equals forty-nine. With Easter Sunday counting as the first Sunday of (the) Easter (Season), the Seventh Sunday of Easter represents a count of forty-three days since Jesus was found not in the tomb. Add another week of days and the number of days adds up to fifty, which is the meaning of "Pentecost" ("The Fiftieth Day").

Again, none of that holds the water of truth or reality, because Christianity enjoys the luxury of ignorance to the ways of the Jews and their predecessors, the Israelites. As a typical Christian, I knew nothing of the "counting of the omer," which is a custom done by Jews during the time period between the beginning of the Passover festival (*Pesach*) and the festival of Weeks (*Shavuot*).

In both Leviticus and Deuteronomy, God told the Israelites to do this:

> "From the day after the Sabbath, the day you brought the sheaf of the wave offering, count off seven full weeks. Count off fifty days up to the day after the seventh Sabbath, and then present an offering of new grain to the Lord." (Leviticus 23:15-16)

> "Count off seven weeks from the time you begin to put the sickle to the standing grain. Then celebrate the Festival of Weeks to the Lord your God by giving a freewill offering in proportion to the blessings the Lord your God has given you. And rejoice before the Lord your God at the place he will choose as a dwelling for his Name—you, your sons and daughters, your male and female servants, the Levites in your towns, and the foreigners, the fatherless and the widows living among you. Remember that you were slaves in Egypt, and follow carefully these decrees." (Deuteronomy 16:9-12)

The second day of the Passover festival is when a "wave offering" was made in the Temple (originally the tabernacle). That means the first wheat grown in the new year was to be collected, with "the sheath" amounting to an "omer" in dry measure. During the eight days of the Passover festival, God told the Israelites: "For seven days present a food offering to the Lord. And on the seventh day hold a sacred assembly and do no regular work." This is the "wave offering" that is ceremoniously done on the second full day of the festival. It is the "offering of the first fruits." This means *Shavuot*, which in Hebrew means "Weeks," is a counting after the ceremony called "*HaBikkurim*" ("first of the harvest") occurs. *Shavuot* is after the counting of fifty days, when the new grains are eaten as a judge of the quality of the first harvest of the year.

The reason the Day of Pentecost is important is it represents the "Fiftieth" (*pentékosté*) day. This numbering to fifty days is more important than a way to determine the quality of early grains. After ten days from escaping from Egypt, Moses had led the Israelites to the base of Mount Sinai. He then spent forty days in a cloud on top of the mountain. On the fiftieth day he brought down the Covenant. This makes the Israelites reflect the "wave offering to the Lord," as the "first fruits" that were cut from the fields of the world (Egypt). Those "first priests" would be ordained when the Laws of Moses were agreed to be their commitment to God (YHWH).

The Passover week occurred in Egypt and the celebration of the First Fruits would occur in the Promised Land (not the wilderness of Sinai). Thus, the counting of fifty days is symbolic of the deaths and rebirths of the Israelite people (Passover – *Pesach*), until they had memorized Mosaic Law as His priests of the true religion (First Fruits – *Shavuot*). Still, that was the state when God sent His Son to reenact this symbolism.

The execution and death of Jesus reflects how he said, "Very truly I tell you, unless a kernel of wheat falls to the ground and dies, it remains only a single seed. But if it dies, it produces many seeds." (John 12:24) This means Easter Sunday reflects "the sheaf of the wave offering," after Jesus appeared as himself resurrected among his disciples and their families. When Jesus stayed and taught them for forty days, "Jesus did many other things as well. If every one of them were written down, I suppose that even the whole world would not have room for the books that would be written." (John 21:25)

That period of time would be when the Law would be written on the hearts of true priests for Yahweh, so that when Jesus Ascended on the forty-ninth day, the true First Fruits of Christianity began speaking from the wisdom of the Holy Spirit on the Fiftieth Day (Pentecost). The ascension of Jesus to be seated at the right hand of God the Father took place on the forty-ninth day (a Sabbath, the seventh of seven Sabbaths), but the Holy Spirit of Jesus was reborn many times over (the vine produced good fruit) on Sunday, the first day of the week (*yom rishon*) – the seventh Sunday of seven Sundays.

Christians **think** that Jesus was raised from death on Easter Sunday, but that is wrong. Jesus, as the Son of God (the Son of Man), was risen after "the third day" of death – Thursday-Friday-**Saturday** – after seventy-two hours dead. As God's Son, he would naturally rise on a Sabbath, the day God deemed holy.

Jesus was discovered raised on Sunday, when Sunday officially began the previous sundown (6:00 PM). That symbolizes when Jesus is discovered risen within each and every true **Christ**ian, as the "wave offering before the Lord." Thus, the seven Sundays of being trained to be just like Jesus is the symbolic meaning of the Easter Season.

The Day of Pentecost then reflects when the good fruit of the vine ceases being immature, unripe, and sour growths that need more teaching (the body and blood of Christ). That day is when the disciples morphed into Apostles and stood up before the hungry and presented themselves as ready to be consumed. The flow of the Holy Spirit through the tongues of those twelve means those seeds also fell to the ground and were planted in three thousand pilgrims in Jerusalem that Fiftieth Day. This means the Day of Pentecost truly belongs in the Easter Season, just as Palm Sunday belongs in the Lenten Season. It brings an end to the counting of one's readiness.

This concept of Pentecost being part of the Easter Season is new to me. It was only recently that I discovered this association to the Easter Season, as I had assumed it beaconed the beginning of the Ordinary Season that is numbered ordinarily as Sundays after Pentecost. Since all those Sundays bear the name "Pentecost," I mistakenly connected that day with the following season. Still, the symbolism is like a circle, when one point reflects both a beginning and an end; so I was not entirely wrong.

The Ordinary Season symbolizes when God's First Priests are divinely ordained to sow to the world. Before one can do that properly, as one inspired by the Holy Spirit, one must be reborn as Jesus (the Son of Man) in one's own body of flesh. Being reborn as Jesus is the theme of the Easter Season and therefore the expected given of the Ordinary Season. The Day of Pentecost, when "like the blowing of a violent wind came from heaven" and "tongues of fire that separated and came to rest on each of them," becomes when the birth of the Christ Mind becomes one with a true **Christ**ian.

Jesus was the Christ (the Messiah) because he was born in possession of that voice of the Father, using only words that came from the Holy Spirit. Normal human beings are born of human brains in temporal bodies of flesh that surround an immortal soul. Lent is when that soul dies of self-importance. Easter is when that soul is reborn as Jesus Christ; and the Ordinary season after Pentecost is when new Jesuses go out into the world in ministry, fully trained to speak only for God.

I feel it is most important to see each season in the liturgical year as like a wall chart, by which to measure one's personal, spiritual growth. Christians are the "little children" chosen by God and it is He who measures our Spiritual growth. Every year we recognize baby Jesus was born on December 25th (when that date is arbitrary and most probably not when God would plan His Son to be born). Every year we see a baby in a trough of hay; but how often in your life do you commemorate a birthday with pictures of a naked baby in his or her first bath? Never! The candles on a birthday cake get more numerous as the years go by. However, we only see baby Jesus at Christmas.

Why?

The reason is Christmas, set near the shortest day of the year, reflects when the Christ child must be born within each and every true **Christ**ian. The recognition is not for baby Jesus in a manger in Bethlehem thousands of years ago, but for the time when God delivered us from our darkest hour and we because Jesus reborn.

Lent is then when we are preparing ourselves (our egos) to die. Without that death, an individual becomes the fulfillment of Jesus saying, "No one can serve two masters. Either you will hate the one and love the other, or you will be devoted to the one and despise the other. You cannot serve both God and possessions." (Matthew 6:24) The use of *"mamona,"* translated as "money" or "possessions," becomes symbolic of an ego taking delight as a soul in the flesh. Therefore, we cannot serve the Spiritual when we lust for the physical.

Lent is when we must choose if we are disciples of Jesus. It is the decision time, as Jesus said, "Whoever wants to be my disciple must deny themselves and take up their cross and follow me." (Matthew 16:24) "Deny self" means the death of an ego (self). We "take up our crosses and follow Jesus," not so much through the persecution to death by crucifixion, but as tendrils of the true vine. Each Christian must be a raised stake upon which the vine of Christ stays away from the ground, where all the maladies that beset good fruit set in (review how Cain was not raised in this manner).

Easter is then a reflection of when each true Christian has given way and let go of one's self-ego, so the baby Jesus inside can become a fully grown adult, as we are. Easter is not so much about remembering how Jesus rose from death and went to prove he was a superman, but remembering in each of us when Jesus spoke to us and we did not recognize it was him.

Easter is when the breath of Jesus breathes into us and we individually open our souls up to "receive the Spirit." Easter Sunday is all about the individual resurrection of

Jesus Christ in new flesh. The Easter Season is then when true Christians are prepared for ministry, by receiving the Christ Mind.

It is most important that one read thes sermons that follow with this mindset about why we listen to sermons during this most important liturgical time of year. Easter is not about having a bunny or chicken that has been died in pastel colors. It is not about when we can wear white clothes. Easter is not about wicker baskets with bright green artificial grass or chocolate bunnies in cardboard boxes. That is serving *mamona*, not God.

Easter and the seven weeks following, including the Day of Pentecost, are all about listening to the risen Lord teaching one how to become Jesus Christ and go out into the world a priest of Yahweh, another Son of God (regardless of one's human gender). Please listen to my words and see if you can hear the voice of God's inspiration. Please read my words and see if you can feel the presence of the Holy Spirit entering your soul. Please read the words I was led to write and see if you can see the resurrection of Jesus Christ talking to you personally.

# Easter Sermons: A Season Named Easter

# EASTER SERMONS

# YEAR A

# EASTER SUNDAY

# YEAR A

**Relevant readings:**
Jeremiah 31:1-6 or
Acts 10:34-43
Psalm 118:1-24
Colossians 3:1-4 or
Acts 10:34-43
Matthew 28:1-10 or
John 20:1-18

## Easter Sunday is time to see and believe

Alleluia, Christ the Lord is risen!

(The Lord has risen indeed!)

# Easter Sermons: Easter Sunday, Year A

I want to welcome all the people who have been away from a physical church so long, as well as all those who regularly gather each Sunday. It is wonderful to have everyone come in celebration that Christ arose from his tomb, almost two thousand years ago.

We represent the current state of a New Covenant that began when a dead man arose after being dead for three days; then coming out of a tomb.

We are the present state, but the future state of Christianity depends on the faith of those today. It does not depend on the faith of those before us.

This is why Easter Sunday is so important. It is when we KNOW this past event occurred, because it has been repeated many times since … in remembrance … up to this point of our remembrance now.

We would not feel the call to be here, in this church or in some other Christian church service, somewhere on Easter Sunday, if we did not believe Jesus arose from the dead.

The true importance of Easter Sunday is that we celebrate the time when Jesus was reborn within each one of us, and within every believer in Jesus Christ. We FEEL the rebirth in us today.

Without that step being taken, of personally FEELING the importance of that Resurrection, nothing changes.

As human beings, we are born of sin. That is not a judgment. That is what all religions teaching of only One God say. As believers of one of those religions, we recognize that every one of us is flawed, impure, defiled ... a sinner ... just because we are human.

We pray to God to forgive us each Sunday. Our faith has us say publicly and collectively, "We humbly repent." All the sins us sinners are prone to do are recognized as having happened by that confession.

We are forgiven, for asking God to wash us clean; but, for that loving act of kindness, in return we are not to remain sinners.

We are supposed to die as sinners and be reborn with the mind of Christ. We are each supposed to have ourselves come back to life as one who no longer sins ... for the rest of our mortal life. We are, each of us individually and all of us collectively, to be Resurrected.

This is why the Apostle Paul wrote to the Colossians, saying, "If you have been raised with Christ, seek things that are above, where Christ is, seated at the right hand of God."

If Easter Sunday means that Christ has risen within you, then seek things that are above.

Do you remember Lent? For those of you who have been absent lately, that season just passed.

That was practice time. Lent is the time to seek one sin that you can master, and not let it master you. By proving yourself for forty days, you raise yourself to a position that allows Jesus to raise you, like he did Lazarus. Lent is the basic training requirement for receiving the spirit to do what it takes next ... to fully sacrifice yourself, your being, your life as a sinner.

Paul went on to say, "Set your minds on things that are above, not on things that are on earth, for you have died, and your life is hidden with Christ in God."

You have died in the sense that your mind is no longer on sin. You have ended that human brain-led existence, replacing it with the mind of Christ. The life you once knew is over. It has become hidden with Christ in God. Your ego just stepped out of the way, and Jesus was reborn into you, because your sins have been hidden in forgiveness.

Finally, Paul wrote, "When Christ **who is your life** is revealed, then you also will be revealed with him in glory."

You will be revealed with him in glory. You will be Jesus at all his best. Jesus will be with you ... as you ... and you with him. You will stop being a failed sinner. Your glory will be through providing the new bodily home for the risen Jesus ... your being.

Paul knew this, because Paul was that. He was speaking from personal experience. He was not making that stuff up.

Saying you believe in Jesus Christ is just so much talk, if the truth is that you are never going to walk the walk. You have to own the personal experience that is forever lasting.

In the Gospel reading today, we read how Peter went into the empty tomb, and John followed a little later. John wrote that "he saw and believed." Likewise, we read the words of John, and through those words our mind's eye lets us see what John saw. And, like John, we too see and believe.

John then continued, writing, "As yet they did not understand the scripture, that he must rise from the dead." They believed that prophecy that had previously made no sense to them. Jesus had risen from the dead, because he was not in the tomb in which they placed his lifeless body, having sealed that tomb with a stone. They saw with their own eyes that Jesus was gone from that tomb. He must be raised from the dead, because his linen wrappings were left behind.

BUT ... they did not understand the scripture, although they saw it had been fulfilled. Likewise, Christians do not understand the scripture, if you do not see how believing Jesus rose from the dead has to become YOU dying and then rising as Jesus.

John said he and Peter went back to their homes. He said, "Mary Magdalene went and announced to the disciples, "I have seen the Lord." In Matthew's Gospel, he said Jesus told Mary, "Go and tell my brothers to go to Galilee; there they will see me."

Jesus had risen, but the story was not over. The disciples were next. They would have Jesus rise in them, after they died and were reborn as Apostles of Christ.

Peter wrote, "Jesus commanded us to preach to the people and to testify that he is the one ordained by God as judge of the living and the dead."

Jesus is the judge of who will be alive with Christ within.

# Easter Sermons: Easter Sunday, Year A

Jesus is the judge of who will die to become the risen Jesus. We have to raise our arm and wave, crying out, "Choose me!"

You do not just say, "I read it and I believe." Jesus has to take over the controls to your thoughts and deeds, for you to truly believe AND understand the scripture. For that, you have to be dead.

Zombies are quite the craze now.

A zombie symbolizes anyone who has his mind set on earthly things. They walk around in a daze, looking for another part of their bodies to be sold to Satan, for one more taste of the good life. A zombie is driven to not see anything but what it lusts after.

In the movies and television shows about zombies, they never show them walking deadly towards a new smart phone. They are never seen terrorizing the innocent for a fat bonus at work. They are never shown driving fancy cars, as they claim ownership of every road they travel.

Zombies are only shown figuratively, as dead bodies mindlessly looking for their next meal. Then …

Plop. There falls an eye. Doesn't matter. Without a Christ mind, you have eyes that cannot see. Death goes on, then …

Plop. There falls an ear. Doesn't matter. Without Jesus reborn within you, you have ears that do not hear.

You see, zombies are dead, but they just won't die.

They have souls that cannot go to Heaven, because they have been sold for earthly things. Their souls were sold for sins.

Peter said, "All the prophets testify about Jesus, saying that everyone who believes in him receives forgiveness of sins through his name."

Using the zombie analogy, zombie sins are forgiven by zombies changing their names to Jesus. Still, there is more to that than just walking around with a "Jesus" name tag on, and body parts still falling off.

You have to be committed to never sinning again. You can only do that by saying, "Goodbye" to your earth-centered zombie brain. You have to let the mind of Christ lead you, forever on.

If you have ever watched a zombie movie, it is vividly clear how you get one to die ... you blow its brain out.

The difference for us is that zombies are not real. Real brains need not get shot by rifles. Real bodies do not necessarily need to be hanged from a tree, or nailed to a cross to die.

Figurative death comes by sacrificing our worldly-lusting brains for a mind that only looks for Heaven. We fear the Lord's judgment, banishment from Heaven, so we are afraid to sin. That is how one truly becomes Christian, beyond being a disciple of the risen Jesus.

Think about being asked by God, "Are you ready to stop

# Easter Sermons: Easter Sunday, Year A

sinning?"

Everyone one of us here today would probably, immediately say, "Yes sir!"

But if God then placed us in a Roman arena, amid a few underfed lions, ones sounding upset at us being there, to hear God saying, "That's the spirit. I knew you had it in you." ...

How many of us pretenders would be screaming out, "Mr. Wizard!" in order to be taken back to our sinful little lives, not really ready to stop thinking about worldly things? We are not ready to die for Jesus!

It is not as easy as we think.

It is not simply a matter of faith.

How many of us come to Bible study here, or spend a few hours each week doing home study? How much work is that?

Wouldn't it be wonderful if all we needed to do to get a Law degree or a Medical degree or to become a big-time music star or movie star was to just believe in lawyers, doctors, singers, and actors? What would you be if it were that easy?

<waving hands apart overhead>

Poof! The magic wand is waved over you and you are what you want to be, just by believing.

If that doesn't work, then you might need to buy some ruby red slippers and click your heels three times, but still ... that's not too much to ask, is it?

As Peter and John went home, and as the disciples went to Galilee to meet the risen Jesus, they had believed in Jesus for three years, but they were not ready to become Jesus.

They needed more training.

They needed to take this forgiven of sins stuff seriously.

They had to make an effort to learn how to sacrifice themselves, how to stop desiring things on the worldly plane, and how to receive the spirit of Christ.

They needed forty days of intensive training with the risen Jesus, so he could then ascend and take his seat at the right hand of God.

From above, Jesus could send the Lord's Holy Spirit to those whose minds were only on things above. To receive the Holy Spirit, the old disciples had to die. They had to be reborn as Jesus ... times twelve.

Before, they believed but they did not yet understand one scripture. After the Ascension, they understood ALL the scriptures ... more than could ever be written in any books. A brain cannot reach that level of understanding ... without it being ignited from within, by the Mind of Christ.

There is plenty of Jesus to go around. Who will be willing to die for that?

# Easter Sermons: Easter Sunday, Year A

Amen

# SECOND SUNDAY OF EASTER

# YEAR A

**Relevant readings:**
Acts 2:14, Acts 2:22-32
Psalm 16
1 Peter 1:3-9
John 20:19-31

## The countdown to being an Easter graduate has begun

We are in the Easter Season. We can all wear white clothes, white shoes, white accessories, and even straw hats, from now until Labor Day.

In Sewanee, Tennessee, at the University of the South, the

## Easter Sermons: Second Sunday of Easter, Year A

male students maintain a tradition of wearing seersucker suit jackets and bow ties. This attire can be seen accompanying short pants and sneakers, as tour groups are led around the campus. It is like after Easter year round there.

For anyone who bought the children baby chicks, ducks, or rabbits for Easter Sunday's gift basket ... now is the time to gather some recipes for the aforementioned ... or let them go free in the yard.

In a way, some things that have a traditional association with Easter are comforting, if not cute. Some identify with the Old South ... the Bible belt. Others are representative of pagan celebrations gaining acceptance, as being somewhat parallel to Christian tradition, in order to attract more worshipers.

Unfortunately, none of the fashion or livestock traditions have anything to do with the true meaning of the Easter Season.

It is time we refreshed our memories about this season.

Today is the Second Sunday of Easter, and there are seven Sundays in all, leading to the Day of Pentecost. The Day of Pentecost begins the longest liturgical season of each year – the Proper Season.

The word "Pentecost" means "fiftieth day." The seven weeks of Easter means forty-nine days come before the fiftieth day, since seven times seven equals forty-nine.

The fiftieth day is a Jewish tradition, which always follows the Passover season. Keeping track of the days to get to that end is called the "Counting of the Omer." An "omer" is a unit of dry measure, which is 9.3 cups, or about .58 a gallon (2.32 quarts).

The Passover festival is a eight-day holiday, beginning with the Feast of Unleavened Bread. This is also called the Seder meal and the Jews observe two such meals, one on the evening that begins the festival and the other the evening following the first full day of the Passover. The first and last days of the week-long event are observed as "legal holidays and as holy days involving abstention from work, special prayer services, and holiday meals." (Wikipedia)

The Passover begins, in the Jewish calendar, on the 15th of the month of Nisan. According to Wikipedia, "Passover is a spring festival, so the 15th day of Nisan begins on the night of a full moon after the northern vernal equinox." That is why Easter changes dates from year to year.

The timing of spring is important, so "to ensure that Passover did not start before spring, the tradition in ancient Israel held that the first day of Nisan would not start until the barley was ripe, being the test for the onset of spring."

An omer of barley was brought to the Temple on the second day of the Passover, the 16th of Nisan, and they would begin a countdown to the fiftieth day, which began the Festival of the First Fruits or the Festival of Weeks (a.k.a. *Shavuot*).

These celebrations were not based on styles and trends, but on commandments of the LORD. As such, the forty-nine days also correspond with the time it took Moses to lead the children of Israel from captivity to their agreement with

Easter Sermons: Second Sunday of Easter, Year A

YAHWEH, at the foot of Mt. Horeb in the Sinai.

On the fiftieth day, the children of Israel accepted God as their King. They were the first fruits of the LORD, as priests who would maintain the Covenant with God forever more. In return, God would forever protect His people and offer them the eternity of Heaven.

As Christians, we accept this history as pertinent to our faith. It is from that history that a New Covenant with the LORD came, through Jesus Christ.

When we say, "New Testament," that does not mean the "Old Testament" is thrown out with the bath water. Perhaps, it would be best to say, the Master Covenant came through Moses, with the First Amendment to that Covenant coming through Jesus Christ.

The fact the two are not separate can be seen when Jesus said he came only for the Jews. As such, all of his disciples were Jewish; and they were to be the key elements of Jesus' ministry. The Acts of the Apostles focuses on those beginnings, which came during the festivals when dedicated Jews honored their commitment to the Covenant by going to Jerusalem.

Today, we read of Peter speaking to the crowd that had gathered in Jerusalem to celebrate *Shavuot*, which is the Festival of the First Fruits ... when the omer of barley had passed its test in the Temple. Peter stood as one of twelve newly commissioned Apostles of Christ, the first fruits of the Holy Spirit from Christ, telling the people Jesus was the Messiah. That was on the fiftieth day – the Day of Pentecost.

In John's Gospel, we read of the first day of the week, Sunday, as being when the resurrection was **realized**. The Passover week had just finished. The week's processes had begun on Friday, the 14th of Nissan, with that being the day of preparation for the two Passover Seder meals – one observed on the Sabbath evening and the other observed after the Sabbath had ended, on Sunday. That was when the Last Supper was.

That meal began at 6:00 PM, at the end of a Jewish *Shabbat*. That time officially began the 16th of Nisan, meaning the sacraments of the bread and the wine last shared by Jesus with his disciples took place when Sunday (the first day of the week - *yom rishon*) had begun.

The next morning, after Jesus had been arrested, the first grain harvest of spring was officially placed in the Temple and the Counting of the Omer begun. Likewise, Jesus was (in addition to being prepared to be the Paschal Lamb) the first measure of grains awaiting judgment. Passover week ended on the following Sabbath, which was the 22nd of Nisan. This means Easter Sunday occurred on 23 Nissan, the eighth day of the Counting of the Omer.

Easter Sunday began the first week of the seven weeks of the Easter season. Jesus appeared to Mary Magdalene that morning. He appeared to Cleopas and another follower of Jesus on their way home to Emmaus (his wife Mary) later that afternoon. For a third time, Jesus appeared in the house where ten of eleven disciples were hidden behind a locked door; and, he reappeared later that evening when all eleven disciples were present and accounted for. Jesus made that appearance on day's evening, before sunset, so

# Easter Sermons: Second Sunday of Easter, Year A

all were on Sunday, the first day of the week (*yom rishon*).

John told us that Thomas was not present for that First Sunday of Easter meeting in the house. To some, a misreading of John's Gospel makes them think Jesus reappeared before the eleven on the Second Sunday of Easter – "a week later." That would seem to be the 30th of Nisan, the 15th day of the counting of the omer. However, because Christians do not maintain this counting of the days, it is easy to misread the translations of the Greek into English.

The first day of that Passover festival was a Sabbath, the day of the LORD. Jesus was figuratively presented to the Temple as the sacrificial lamb on God's day. Why would God plan that any other way?

The first Sunday of the Passover week (16 Nissan), Jesus was harvested and prepared to be presented to the Temple as a measure of spring barley. The Counting of the Omer would begin, with Jesus being just a measured sample of the plenty that would come. Jesus was the first fruit of God on earth to be tested.

On the last day of the Passover festival, also the Sabbath – the day of the LORD – Jesus was freed from the bondage of the physical realm, having been dead for three days. Why would Jesus **not** go into the hands of his Father on the Lord's Day?

The second Sunday since the beginning of the Passover is the first Sunday of Easter (23 Nissan), when Jesus was risen, to begin a New phase for those dedicated to the One God.

The third Sunday since the beginning of Passover is the second Sunday of Easter (30 Nisan), when Jesus supposedly met with the eleven disciples, including Thomas, as part of their in-depth training as would-be Apostles. However, in terms of the Counting of the Omer, 30 Nisan would be day 15 of 50. Knowing Jesus spent forty days with his disciples and ascended on the forty-ninth day means that would have been impossible on that date.

Examining the actual Greek text bring truth to bear.

In actuality, John wrote in Greek, "*Kai meth' hēmeras oktō*," which is an important statement (introduced by a capitalized "*Kai*") that translates to state, "after days eight." To interpret that as "a week later" only shows one's ignorance of the omer count. This means the "days" were those counted and "eight" was the day designated on that day. Since the omer count began on Nisan 16, the actual Jewish date was Nisan 23.

The Passover ended on a *Shabbat*, Nisan 22, making Sunday (the first day of the week) be Nisan 23 and that was when Thomas saw Jesus, meaning Jesus appeared twice in the locked room on the same day (once when Thomas was away and once when Thomas was there).

John wrote of what followed that second meeting in the house: "Now Jesus did many other signs in the presence of the disciples." Jesus would spend forty days meeting with his disciples, giving them assignments and lessons, beginning two days later, on Tuesday, the tenth day after the counting of the omer began.

Jesus would Ascend to Heaven on the 50th day following

Easter Sermons: Second Sunday of Easter, Year A

the first day of Passover (15 Nisan to 5 Sivan), a Sabbath, the day of the LORD. Why would the Lord plan for His Son to Ascend on any day other than the Lord's Day?

The disciples would be raised as Apostles on the 50th day of the Counting of the Omer, a Sunday (6 Sivan).

Can you see the blending of Judaism with Christianity?

The Sabbath has always remained the day of the LORD. Sunday has always remained the first day of the week; but, as Christians, we represent the first light of the New Revelation that the Christ has come.

We are here on the first day of the week! The symbolism of the first day, in Genesis terms, is "In the beginning God created heaven and earth." While we are still living the "God day" that is the Sabbath (made holy by religion's presence), God created a highest form of religious being that would be the fruit of His Son.

Look at your calendars at home. Sunday is the first day and Saturday is the seventh day. Saturday is the Sabbath, the Lord's Day.

We are here today ... Sunday ... because we bring ourselves to the light of the Son, for him to shine on us, within us, and from us.

That is the meaning of the Easter Season. We have to let peace be with us.

Three times in John's Gospel, he quoted Jesus saying, "Peace be with you."

<Raise two fingers as a hippie peace sign>

**PEACE!**

That is not what Christ meant by saying, "Peace be with you."

We think of "peace" as not being angry, not being at war, as Kumbaya, where we all get along well together. We think of it as a greeting, without deep meaning.

When Jesus first said, "Peace be with you," the disciples were behind a locked door because they were possessed by "fear of the Jews." Fear is a lack of peace. Thus, "peace" can be defined as, "Inner contentment; serenity." Peace means "Do not be afraid."

John said the disciples rejoiced at being put at ease by Jesus, at which point Jesus repeated that instruction, adding, "As the Father has sent me, so I send you."

That is our mission! We are to be sent by Jesus, just as God sent Jesus to show us how to be sent.

Then John said Jesus "breathed on them and said, "Receive the Holy Spirit."

That is the only way to become sent! You have to receive the purpose.

Then Jesus added, "If you forgive the sins of any, they are forgiven them; if you retain the sins of any, they are retained."

# Easter Sermons: Second Sunday of Easter, Year A

This was a statement about fearing those who sin. In that instance, it was the "Jews," whom the disciples had locked the door to keep out. The Jews killed Jesus, and the disciples feared they could be, might be, and may be likewise the focus of some yet materialized sins, by the Jews.

We have our own people to stop being afraid of, who are always the powers that are one with us, but who wield the sword of sin over our heads as our enemies, threatening us not to do anything holy.

Jesus said forgive and forget. Let's move on. I have bigger plans for you; and to "Receive the Holy Spirit," you cannot be cloaked in fear. You have to have peace within.

This is what the Easter Season should be about: Losing the fears that keep one from receiving the Holy Spirit.

There are seven weeks to have Jesus be reborn within you. Seven weeks to be raised in faith. Seven weeks to prepare for the fiftieth day, the Day of Pentecost, when the Holy Spirit turns followers of Jesus into the Apostles in Christ.

When we reach that point we can look back, as did Peter, who wrote about all the trials and tribulations a believer of Christ will have to face. Peter wrote, "You have had to suffer various trials, so that the genuineness of your faith ... is tested by fire."

If you are still afraid, then a test of fire will have you run away from serving God. If you still have fears, you will flinch when someone demands you prove your faith. If you are hiding behind locked doors, fearful of someone knowing what you believe, then you will deny having ever known Jesus.

Peter wrote, "Although you have not seen Jesus, you love him. Even though you do not see him now, you believe in him." That is what an Apostle comes to realize.

Seeing is not believing. **BEING** is believing!

Thomas would become an Apostle, but while still a disciple he said, "Unless I see the mark of the nails in his hands, and put my finger in the mark of the nails and my hand in his side, I will not believe."

That prompted Jesus to ask, "Have you believed because you have seen me? Blessed are those who have not seen and yet have come to believe."

Not seeing, but believing means **BEING** Jesus reborn!

Imagine Jesus asking you, "Have you come here today to see me and to feel the Holy Spirit, because otherwise you will not believe?"

There is work still to be done before graduation day arrives.

Peace be with you, so you may receive the spirit.

Amen

# Easter Sermons: Second Sunday of Easter, Year A

# THIRD SUNDAY OF EASTER

# YEAR A

**Relevant readings:**
Acts 2:14, Acts 2:36-41
Psalm 116:1-17
1 Peter 1:17-23
Luke 24:13-35

## We all walk the road to Emmaus and never recognize Jesus is with us too, waiting to be invited in to stay

In terms of the Christian liturgical calendar, today is the 14th day of the Easter season, counting toward the fiftieth day, our Day of Pentecost.

Easter Sermons: Third Sunday of Easter, Year A

In terms of the Jewish calendar, they maintain a ritual called the Counting of the Omer. An "omer" is a dry measure, which is a sample of first barley grain reaped in the spring. It is ceremoniously presented to the Temple priests on the second day of the Passover festival week. They then daily announce the count, as ritual custom paralleling the days from the release of the children of Israel from Egypt, until Moses brought down the Law. Each day of freedom, leading to the pact between them and God, is recounted each year, until they have recreated the fiftieth day, the day called Pentecost (which is Greek for "Fiftieth" day).

Since the Jewish Passover week lasts parts of eight days, with the first Christian Easter Sunday - the first day of the week – being the first day after the Passover week ended, then Christian Easter Sunday was actually the 7th day of the Jewish Counting of the Omer. This means the Jewish Pentecost (the real 50th day) comes a week sooner than ours.

According to the Jewish (real) count, today is the 21st day of the counting to 50, not the 14th.

But, who's counting?

If you carefully ponder the words from today's reading in Acts, you realize that Peter was talking to Jews. He spoke to them on the Jewish Day of Pentecost, in Jerusalem. All those Jews were there for another festival, one two days in length, called *Shavuot*.

The Festival of Weeks (the meaning of *Shavuot*) begins 50 days after the feast of the First Fruits, which always takes place on Nissan 16, the second day of the Festival of the

Unleavened Bread. The day of the Feast is the day the Counting of the Omer begins.

Peter raised his voice for a large crowd of Jews, so they could all hear. Peter called them all "Brothers."

Peter told the Jews coming into Jerusalem for a festival commanded by God, in His Covenant between Himself and the children of Israel:

> "The promise of a Messiah is for you, for your children, and for all who are far away," those Jews scattered to the far reaches of the known world.

Peter influenced 3,000 Jews to believe their Messiah had indeed come. I doubt 3,000 Gentiles (i.e. Romans) would have known what Peter was talking about.

Peter was still speaking primarily to the Jews, those who had begun the first Christian churches in the Middle East, when he wrote his first letter of encouragement, asking them to "hang in there" against growing persecution.

Peter wrote, "Live in reverent fear during the time of your exile." They were in exile from the Jews who did not accept that a Messiah had come. The new Christian-Jews were encouraged to fear God more than human beings of any denomination.

Peter went on to say, "You know that you were ransomed from the futile ways inherited from your ancestors." Their "ancestors" were the Jews who lost the land they once enjoyed, causing all Jews to be exiled, even in Jerusalem. The Jews who believed in Jesus were being "ransomed," where the price they had to pay was their own blood. Their blood was sacrificed through the persecution of other Jews and those ruling all the lands those Jews lived in.

In a way, Peter was telling his Jewish-Christian "brothers," "Life's hard, then you die. Hang in there. Don't give up."

Peter wrote, "Love one another deeply from the heart. You have been born anew, through the living and enduring word of God."

So, if you caught that during the reading … that Peter was focused on the Jews more than the Gentiles, because the Jews were being persecuted for being Christians by Jews … then where do we Gentile Christians fit in?

Well, in the Book of Acts, Peter did add something about "all others." He said, "The promise is for … everyone whom the Lord our God calls to him."

The "promise" is for sins to be forgiven, if people repent, and become baptized in the name of Jesus Christ.

But, the "promise" is not a one-way street. The "promise" had long existed between the Israelites and God, based on the agreement made when Moses came down with the commandments. The "promise" was agreed upon, that the Jews had to follow God's Commandments and a number of laws. Christians can have the same "promise," with a clause that says, "as long as you honor the Lord God eternally," and believe Jesus is the Messiah "promised" to the Jews.

Peter said the Jews were "ransomed … with the precious blood of Christ, like that of a lamb without defect or blemish." The lamb without defect or blemish is a statement about the "kidnapper" being that darned agreement, where the ransom is the "eternal" part of that Covenant. Once chosen by God, one is always expected to meet one's end of the "promise."

Jesus is the sacrificial lamb that frees everyone from sins. Jesus died just like many woolly firstling lambs were sacrificed, whose blood was then spread over the doorways of the chosen ones, to free the Israelites from Egypt.

Just because you jump onto the Christ wagon as a Gentile does not mean you are not also "ransomed." The reward you seek is held in Heaven, until you pay up. You have responsibilities that must be upheld.

So what if the Jews keep up with their end of the agreement, to always keep track of the dates and times of commanded festivals and celebrations? They signed up for that responsibility. We didn't ... right?

If we Gentile Christians want to be a week later in the start of our count, go for it! No need to count a measure of barley. It is better to count the number of days since Jesus was resurrected, right?

Just realize the eternal aspect that comes along with any agreement you enter into with the Easter Christ. Just like the Jews, you have to seek to be filled with the Holy Spirit. Just like the Jews, you have to commit to explaining scripture to those who do not yet understand.

When Peter wrote to the Christian Jews and told them they had "inherited the futile ways of your ancestors," those trivial and useless ways were found popping up all throughout the Gospels. That followed all the miserable failure found throughout the Old Testament ... until the Promised Land was forever lost. The Jews who believed in Jesus as the Messiah, thus the first Christians, inherited a legacy that said, "If you do not hold up your end of the bargain, then there is no promise."

The Pharisees had carried a torch of ineptitude, seeking to regain glory lost. However, they were not teaching anyone to be good and sin free.

They didn't know how.

That meant the people grumbled about the hypocrisy; but the people never dared do anything about it. Everything about the Second Temple was a shell of what the original intent was. That was why Jesus came.

Everyone was out for himself. Everyone did what it took to get by; but, just to be on the safe side, everyone played the role of believer in God. The laws did set forth expectations: to learn the Torah and pay some tithes; so they tried to memorize text and give money.

When Jesus began his ministry, he travelled the lands of Judea and Galilee for three years. He opened some eyes and ears, while doing some miraculous healing too.

Then he died. He was unfairly killed; but Jesus had said Jerusalem was the city that killed its prophets.

Last week we read about doubting Thomas. He would not believe Jesus had come back to life after three days dead, unless he saw it for himself. Only if he physically touched the wounds in Jesus' body would he believe.

Today, we read the story of Jesus appearing as a stranger on the road to Emmaus, as he walked and talked with Cleopas and wife, relatives of Jesus and Mary.

Cleopas told Jesus all about how it was discovered that Jesus was not in his tomb, and that some of the women said they saw angels there.

But, Cleopas added, "They did not see him." I imagine the rumour that his disciples stole his body, to make it seem he had resurrected, had already begun.

Cleopas was saying, in essence, "You know stranger ... it is kinda hard to believe that. Just because someone said it, doesn't make it true. Even if it is someone you know and trust ... someone you love very much."

"You want it to be true, but ... three days dead!?!? Then he came back to life and disappears?!?!?! Come on. That just does not happen."

"They said it was so ... but I can only say what they said. I cannot confirm the rumour."

Jesus, appearing as a stranger, went off on Cleopas, his uncle, brother of his father Joseph.

"Oh? So what then? Did you ever see the prophets who wrote the books you say you believe in? Did you ever see God?"

Easter Sermons: Third Sunday of Easter, Year A

"Is seeing believing?" Jesus asked, in essence.

The rest of the walk to Emmaus finds Jesus telling Cleopas and Mary about every prophecy written, telling about Jesus living, dying, and resurrecting JUST LIKE IT HAPPENED.

Cleopas and Mary were amazed.

Their hearts were deeply touched by what was written and the meaning that was clearly there. They knew all the scriptures, but they had never before realized any of what this stranger had just told them.

When the three reached Emmaus, Cleopas and Mary headed to their home. Jesus kept walking down the road.

They asked Jesus to stay with them. It was late, and would be dark in a couple of hours. "Stay with us, they asked him," Luke wrote.

They wanted him to tell them more about the meaning of scripture. Jesus could sleep over and then hit the road the next morning. Cleopas and Mary wanted this stranger to stay longer with them.

They knew the stranger was a rabbi, because he knew so much. That has to be why they asked a stranger into their home and then asked him to break the bread and bless the meal.

When Jesus broke the bread, blessed it and handed it to them, their eyes were opened and they saw it was Jesus.

But, at that point he vanished from sight.

Robert Tippett

In the practice of Zen Meditation, the objective is to reach Nirvana. However, by the time you think you have reached Nirvana, you are no longer there.

Cleopas and Mary reached a similar point of feeling. They said to each other, "Our hearts were burning within us while he was talking to us on the road, while he was opening the scriptures to us."

Today, when we celebrate the Eucharist, when you hear how Jesus broke the bread and said, "Take, eat, this is my Body, which is given for you. Do this in remembrance of me," realize this means: Read scripture and remember Jesus was prophesied. Read as if you are on the road to Emmaus.

The body of Christ is the Holy Bible. The mind of Christ opens eyes and ears to the meaning of that bread, that sustenance.

If you walk the road of Bible study, and if you say you believe in the Holy Bible, but you hear yourself saying …

"You know … there are a lot of people better educated than me … I just can't see all the things they say is there."

"I trust **them** to know, and I love **them**, so I believe **they** mean well, but …."

"Unless **I see** what it means with **my** own two eyes …."

Excuses, excuses, excuses … they take you away, so far from that which is "promised" in your agreement with God.

# Easter Sermons: Third Sunday of Easter, Year A

Let your ears hear Jesus tell you, "Oh, how foolish you are, and how slow of heart to believe all that the prophets declared!"

If you do not eat the bread, then how can you be thirsty enough to drink the wine?

The wine represents the blood of the unblemished sacrificial lamb, who shed his blood for you and for many, the blood of the new covenant. Jesus shed it so it would course through your veins and arteries, filling you with deep spiritual awakening. You have to act and digest the body first.

This is the countdown to the Pentecost, the Fiftieth day.

The disciples turned from weak-kneed, fearful doubters into full-fledged Apostles, filled with the Holy Spirit, converting 3,000 pilgrims in a single sermon.

The purpose of the season is to become a matured fruit of the living vine. You must **want** that first fruit emotion burning within your heart, so you **want** to immediately run and tell your friends.

You have to do something that welcomes Jesus to come into your home – your body of flesh. You have to recognize the superior knowledge of the Christ Mind, so you want Jesus to break and bless the bread – to invite Jesus Christ into your mind.

You have to eat the bread and receive the spirit.

No one can do it for you; but you need higher help. That help can come from outside one's being.

The responsibility is yours alone, however, as part of the New Covenant with God, in the name of Christ. Being "in the name" means being reborn as Jesus and the Christ Mind, both sent via God's Holy Spirit.

That is all one needs to have the strength to walk away from sin and walk the road of righteousness. Then you can explain scripture to strangers, looking nothing like Jesus.

Amen

# Easter Sermons: Third Sunday of Easter, Year A

# FOURTH SUNDAY OF EASTER

# YEAR A

**Relevant readings:**
Acts 2:42-47
Psalm 23
1 Peter 2:19-25
John 10:1-10

## When you understand Jesus is the gate-keeper AND the gate, then it is time to go "all-in"

Today represents the end of the fourth week of the counting of the Omer.

We are now on the 28th day since the ceremonial presentation of the First Fruits in the Temple during the Feast of the Unleavened Bread – Passover (Nisan 16). That count reflects the one done by God's chosen people, the Jews.

The count is 22 for us Christians, since Easter Sunday. We have now begun the fourth week of the symbolic training that the disciples experienced with the risen Lord.

Some Jews, those following in the footsteps of the descendants of the servants to the Temple priest, the Levites, see the number four as representing "Foundations."

Such symbolic associations are Kabbalistic, and they bear importance, upon which is worthy of spending a moment of reflection.

The four corners of the earth means going in all directions, with everything covered. There are four elements of the material universe: Earth, Water, Air, and Fire. From those elements, everything in the physical realm is made.

We say we want to be "fair and square," where the meaning reflects rules, honesty, and a solid footing, where stability is in focus.

The cornerstone, or foundation stone, is a four-sided cube, upon which we build from strength and stability. Thus, Jesus is the earthly cornerstone to Heaven.

So, the fourth number in the counting of weeks (*Shavuot* is the Festival of Weeks, beginning with the Day of Pentecost) can be seen as focusing on readings that set the Foundation for belief in Christ.

In John's Gospel, we hear Jesus tell of such foundation, using the analogy of a sheepfold. Jesus said he was the gate keeper to that pen or enclosure for sheep, where multiples of different flocks would spend the night. But, Jesus also said he was the gate itself.

The Israelites, then Jews, were the focus of that analogy, where the Law of Moses acted as the surrounding stones creating the sheep enclosure. Like the Jews, we Christians are the "sheep" in the same "pen." As Episcopalians – our flock's title – we are but one of many flocks that fall under the heading of "Christianity."

Each congregation of each individual church can then be seen as but one flock among many flocks, in a very large holding area.

Jesus opens the gate to the pen, into which all believers in Christ enter; but Jesus opens the gate to good shepherds. Those are the people who have become the mind of Christ, through receipt of the Holy Spirit – his Apostles. They send in their flocks of sheep to Christ for safekeeping.

Those good shepherds are Apostles, but the Apostles were first sheep, who had a Good Shepherd.

When one sees the ultimate purpose of Christianity to be something like, "Tag, you've got It," where "It" is the Holy Spirit, then the sheepfold is actually the place where Apostles are formed. It is from that place that Jesus becomes the "gate" to Heaven, for the Apostles.

Jesus said, "There are many rooms in my Father's house," and he has gone there to prepare a place for us sheep, with the expectation that we will become Apostles.

We are not the only ones in the pen, waiting for that development. Remember, we are on day 22, so there is time left before the Fiftieth Day arrives. Still, there is much work to do.

As I said, there are many flocks in the sheepfold of Christ. At the time of the first Apostles, only Jewish people believed Jesus was their Messiah. Jesus resurrected and spent time with his disciples, teaching them how their role was to become Apostles. He then ascended, leaving them to be filled with the Holy Spirit. With Jesus watching in spirit, the disciples were elevated to Apostles, through their hard work, becoming Good Shepherds for both Jews and Gentiles.

Other flocks are now in the sheepfold, making up the universal [catholic] church, of which Episcopalians are a part.

Every denomination is represented in this enclosure of Christianity. As long as they enter with Christ opening the gate, and they see Christ as the gate to the Father, they have the opportunity to be more.

This then turns the focus on the Good Shepherds, those who have gathered flocks of sheep. Jesus said, "The flock will not follow a stranger, but will run from one unknown. A Good Shepherd calls his own sheep by name, and the sheep know the sound of the Good Shepherd's voice."

This says an Apostle is one from the flock. He or she is one in a family relationship with the flock. He or she is one who has a personal investment with the flock, based on love, caring, and a burning desire to have each sheep in the flock to grow itself into an Apostle, being able to lead a flock of its own.

We tend to look at a priest, a vicar, a rector, pastor, minister or preacher as a good shepherd; and that is the way it most definitely should be, but ...

Each Christian family is its own church, with its own Good Shepherd.

If one looks around the pews of any Christian church on any Sunday, one can see the different flocks of that individual church. In that way, each church building acts as a surrogate sheepfold for Christ ... one of many around the world.

Regardless of where, one should find that a well-raised flock is like a good vine that bears good fruit. An Apostle is then not only a Good Shepherd, but also a Good Gardener, one who raises the vine off the ground, who pulls out the weeds and wild grapevines that try to intermingle with the good vine. A Good Gardener is one who prepares for new growth each season, by harvesting the good grapes and making holy wine.

In the reading from the Book of the Acts of the Apostles, we see what a Good Shepherd is. In addition, we see who a Christian sheep is.

We read, "Those who had been baptized devoted themselves to the apostles' teaching and fellowship, to the breaking of bread and the prayers."

# Easter Sermons: Fourth Sunday of Easter, Year A

We read that "Awe came upon everyone."

"All who believed were together and had all things in common; they would sell their possessions and goods and distribute the proceeds to all, as any had need."

It was a wonderful life back then, soon after the first rush of the Holy Spirit into the disciples. We find that "day by day the Lord added to their number those who were being saved."

<PAUSE *to reflect on what was just said*>

They sold everything that wasn't needed ... for the common good of all ... and **that system** "added to their number."

The first Christians were "**all-in**" AND "the Lord added to their number those who were being saved."

A few years ago, after reading this passage from the Book of Acts in a lectionary class, it dawned on me that no one was preaching this aspect of devotion. That thought hit me after the class ended and people were heading to the regular morning church service.

I caught up with the leader of that group as he hurried to get his favored spot in a pew, when his favorite spot in the sheepfold was safeguarded. I asked him, "Whatever happened to that "**all-in**" Church?"

As he hurried away, he turned and looked at me, saying, "That didn't work out too well, did it?"

<PAUSE *to reflect on what was just said*>

Who says it didn't work out? People being saved in increasing numbers didn't work out?

It works out perfectly ... **BUT** ... when you start getting away from the family Church, the flock where the good shepherd knows all the names of the sheep and the sheep all know the voice of their shepherd ... **then** you start letting strangers into the mix ....

Maybe that is what didn't work out too well?

You know that Jesus warned us, "Anyone who does not enter the sheepfold by the gate but climbs in by another way is a thief and a bandit."

That means anyone who bypasses the gatekeeper – Jesus.

That means a stranger in the mix ... one who comes in the cover of darkness, when all the sheep are bedded down to sleep, before the dawn has them back out for the green pastures along with their good shepherd.

Anyone who sees a flock's willingness to share for the common good can see that as an opportunity to steal possessions or rob the flock of its needs.

Some people can claim poor unknown Christians are not having their needs met, because they are more willing to help others than help themselves.

Wolves prey on those innocent lambs by using a slick tongue or sob story to take advantage of Christian charity.

## Easter Sermons: Fourth Sunday of Easter, Year A

Such people are not part of the flock's family, but they start telling the sheep how much need they have, which the flock can help end. They start telling the flock how much the flock needs to give.

Because snake oil salesmen of long ago taught so many Americans to always keep one hand on their wallets, lest they get swindled yet again, it is harder to get more than a meagre gift offering to a drug addict that comes to the church office - babies in tow - pleading how their gas or electricity is going to be shut off if they don't get help. They know to go to the churches for a handout; but they cannot get rich that way ... just another fix.

The real danger is when wolves sneak into the sheepfold and begin acting like sheep. They do such a good job getting the other sheep in the flock to give them recognition that they elevate to shepherd status. While he or she might make lots of money from that position, their real danger is asking their flocks to give forgiveness for sinners ... those who never intend stopping their lives of sin.

All denominations of Christian churches have let these wolves into their flocks. The bad shepherds are devouring the flock by influencing them to not be "**all in**."

If this theft and robbery goes on for too long, then the flock becomes destitute. The wolves in sheep's clothing get rich and they destroy the flock at the same time. The next thing you know, the bad shepherd is saying, "Let's just give 10%. I want you to be able to meet your own needs."

Then you hear people saying, that "**all-in** thing didn't work out too well."

The worst part of that theft and robbery is that bad shepherds are not teaching any sheep how to be filled with the Holy Spirit. That means none of the sheep are progressing spiritually, being enabled to become Apostles as God and Christ plan.

That is why we must understand that the gate to Heaven is Jesus Christ, who also opens the gate to the sheepfold, and blesses good shepherds with the gate to Heaven when they graduate from being a sheep to becoming an Apostle.

We cannot allow that theft to take place. We can allow sin to always exist in the world, but if we stop becoming Apostles the gate to heaven slams shut ... because of our lack of commitment.

Back in the early days of these true churches, where everyone was "**all-in**" and together as family, with known leaders who were Apostles, there was plenty of persecution.

Persecution wears down ordinary people. Ordinary people look for ways out of pain and punishment. They look for someone to say, "It is okay. Just stop sharing all things in common. Keep some for yourself. Take it easier. God and Jesus still love you."

If only Jesus left us a Holy Magic Wand, then we could just pull that out and <poof> there would be no more pain and suffering.

Unfortunately ….

Peter wrote his letters to his flocks of sheep that had been left in the care of Good Shepherds. It was their family members who needed encouragement to stay the course. Peter did not tell them to stop being "**all-in**." He told them to maintain being fully committed to God, through Christ.

Peter said, "It is a credit to you if, being aware of God, you endure pain while suffering unjustly." He told them, "If you endure when you do right and suffer for it, you will have God's approval."

Peter told them that Jesus suffered in the same way. True Christians have gained Christ as their Good Shepherd because they recognize how much Jesus suffered for them.

Peter encouraged the early Christian flocks by saying, "You were going astray like sheep, but now you have returned to the shepherd and guardian of your souls."

In a way, Peter said, "Before Jesus died for your sins, you were only paying 10% and that was not working for you at all. You paid for nothing and got what you paid for."

Jesus sacrificed for Heaven, and so should you. No pain, no gain.

We make things seem more difficult than they really are, some times. Those of a certain age remember times when you were children, when you had so little your life seemed unbearable.

There was not enough food to eat, never any of the latest fashions to wear, and not enough heat in the winter or cool in the summer. There was an economic collapse, followed by a World War. Ordinary things were rationed or impossible to get, so that the needs of our troops were met first, and foremost.

You survived because the family pulled together, brothers helping sisters, parents helping children. Aunts and uncles and cousins working together to help one another have their needs met.

It was hard. There was an awful lot of prayer involved too ...

And it preserved the family through hard times.

Since then, times have relaxed and a time of plenty has made life in America bountiful. We have become used to excess. We have lost touch with what true need is.

We have lost touch with the benefit of sacrifice for family. We have lost touch with the need to spend much time together in the temple of commitment -which is any building or place where two or more gather **in the name of Jesus Christ**.

We have moved so far apart from core family members that it is very difficult to break bread at home and eat with glad and generous hearts.

We seem to be praising God for economic wealth and international prosperity, rather than for the Holy Spirit to give us the strength and knowledge to tend our own garden and pasture our own sheep.

We must remember to stay focused on what is truly important, and not become distracted by all the bells and whistles

Easter Sermons: Fourth Sunday of Easter, Year A

of life on the earthly plane.

That is why we must see the Foundation of Christianity as a responsibility we each must bear. We must learn, so we can teach. We must share with those we know, so we all may be one as a family, recognizing each family is just like us.

We are heading toward the Day of Ascension, when Jesus became the gate to Heaven. We are heading toward our Day of Pentecost, when we can make our own personal Covenant with the LORD, so we can be filled with the Holy Spirit. It will be a time when we will see just how well an **"all-in"** system works. We will then begin preparing our garden to bear good fruit, as Apostles.

We are lost without family. We are found by good shepherds. We are taught to become good shepherds. We are called to serve that role, as models of Jesus. We know how "all-in" family must be.

For that reason, we can understand how the shepherd king, David, also fulfilled this role in the same manner. He was a shepherd, a student and a teacher. He knew the full meaning of the song he wrote:

> The LORD is my shepherd; I shall not want.
>
> He makes me lie down in green pastures and leads me beside still waters.
>
> He revives my soul and guides me along right pathways for his Name's sake.
>
> Though I walk through the valley of the shadow of

death, I shall fear no evil; for you are with me; and your rod and your staff, they comfort me.

You spread a table before me; you have anointed my head with oil, and my cup is running over.

Surely your goodness and mercy shall follow me all the days of my life, and I will dwell in the house of the LORD forever.

Amen

# Easter Sermons: Fourth Sunday of Easter, Year A

# FIFTH SUNDAY OF EASTER

# YEAR A

**Relevant readings:**
Acts 7:55-60
Psalm 31:1-5, 15-16
1 Peter 2:2-10
John 14:1-14

## Jesus went to prepare a room in the Father's house, but do you have room in yourself for Jesus?

This is the fifth Sunday in a counting of seven. We are 35 days towards the Christian Pentecost. We have two more weeks to prepare to become Apostles.

# Easter Sermons: Fifth Sunday of Easter, Year A

Today, we see the difference between true faith – total belief in God – and the "I want to believe" kind of watered down faith.

In the counting of the omer, which began the first day the children of Israel were set free by the Pharaoh, and ended when Moses came down from Mount Sinai with the tablets stating the Law of God, 50 days passed.

They wanted to have faith that Moses was talking to God; and the Israelites wanted to believe Moses knew where they were going. But, we all know how that went.

Complain, complain, and complain, then a miracle. Followed by more of the same – complain until another miracle.

When we complain to God, at least we believe in God; but we complain because our hearts are troubled. We are afraid things are not going to get better. We fear the worst. We doubt.

In the Gospel of John, we hear Jesus tell his slightly drunk disciples it is time for him to go to his Father's house. They misunderstand where his Father lives. They want Jesus to go to Google Maps and print out some directions for them, so they can find his house after Jesus leaves them.

Jesus said, "I am the way."

He said, "I will come back to get you and take you to my Father's house."

What do you think that means ... assuming no one here

today is slightly drunk from wine, and you are clear-headed disciples of Jesus?

Before you start to answer that question, let me give you a hint.

We are sitting in a church building that is named after the star character in the reading from the Book of the Acts of the Apostles. [In 2015, my wife's church was name St. Stephen's.]

The book tells of "Acts," not "Inactions."

Stephen was not one of the slightly drunk disciples that were with Jesus at the Last Supper, when Jesus told them he was going to his Father's house to prepare a place for them. He was a deacon who was filled with the Holy Spirit by one of the Apostles. He is considered the first martyr of the Apostles, yet he probably never got to know Jesus, the man, personally, as a disciple.

Stephen, once filled with the Holy Spirit ... once he experienced his own personal Pentecost, or Fiftieth Day ... learned the truth. The truth was from his belief in God and his faith in Jesus as the Christ. That made Stephen stand up and defend that truth.

Stephen acted because the Holy Spirit was within him.

Stephen preached like Jesus at the Temple. The Jews, the same ones who had plotted to kill Jesus; they did the same to Stephen, only quicker.

Stephen was killed because of his faith in God and his be-

Easter Sermons: Fifth Sunday of Easter, Year A

lief in Jesus as the Christ.

Just as Jesus told the disciples, in particular Phillip and Thomas, "I will come back and get you to take you to my Father's house," he fulfilled that promise with Stephen.

Stephen looked up and saw God, the Father, with Jesus at His right hand. They made their presence known.

It so delighted Stephen, he exclaimed to his killers, "Look!"

Instead of looking, "They covered their ears, and with a loud shout all rushed together against" Stephen.

"Look! I see the Father's house, and there is Jesus returning to take me there!"

The Jews didn't care. "Na na na na na … I'm not listening."

We read in Acts how the Jews tossed their coats on the ground, at the feet of Saul (who would become Paul), as they stoned Stephen to death.

Stephen, just like Jesus had done on the cross, asked God to forgive his persecutors. Just as Jesus commended his spirit unto God, quoting from the reading today in Psalm 31, Stephen did the same. Stephen commended his spirit unto Jesus. Both of their spirits left their human bodies for the Father's house … Heaven.

You see, the answer to the question, "What does it mean when Jesus said, "I will return to take you back to the Father's house" is more than simply seeing Jesus' spirit at the right hand of God as death approaches ...

as much as it means Jesus came back **as** Stephen.

The mind of Christ took over for that man of trembling faith and little belief, and transformed Stephen into Jesus – a duplicated model.

A while back, we read of the transformation of Cleopas and his wife Mary, who walked with Jesus on the road home to Emmaus.

They did not recognize Jesus in body, and they were relatives of Jesus and his mother Mary. They knew Jesus more than any others ...from a baby until a grown thirty-something years old man.

But they did not recognize Jesus when he walked that road with them, when Jesus explained how all the scriptures told of the Messiah having been prophesied ... to be exactly as Jesus' life unfolded.

They were amazed.

When we read John recalling Jesus saying, "Let not your hearts be troubled," Cleopas and Mary recognized Jesus when he broke the bread, and they recalled how warm and settled their hearts were.

They **ACTED** at that point. They went back to tell the others.

People could not recognize Stephen as Jesus.

# Easter Sermons: Fifth Sunday of Easter, Year A

In a way, it wasn't Jesus. It was Stephen, the Jew who was born and lived, with relatives and friends, all who knew him as he grew up and lived as Stephen.

Then, suddenly, he became some crazy Jew who did not **ACT** like Stephen had prior. He **ACTED** like Jesus. Stephen was killed because the Jews in the Temple recognized Jesus had returned.

Jesus, as Stephen, forgave the Jews again.

Now, when whoever it was that walked with Cleopas and Mary on the road to Emmaus stopped being Jesus …

when Jesus suddenly disappeared … they were transformed. Their hearts were at peace. Their faith was elevated. Their belief in Jesus … not just as a prophet … but as their Messiah … was uplifted and uplifting.

They **ACTED** as changed people. Jesus disappeared from before them and became them.

Now, think of the man named Saul.

He was a young man, the son of a Pharisee, probably watching his daddy hurl killer rocks as someone judged a blasphemer.

We know from Paul's letters that he was converted by a vision of Jesus, asking him, "Saul, why do you persecute me?" But, as a young man watching a man be stoned to death, that **ACT** must have had some effect on him, leaning him towards that conversion.

John wrote that Jesus said, "Very truly I tell you, unless a kernel of wheat falls to the ground and dies, it remains only a single seed. But if it dies, it produces many seeds."

Stephen was one kernel of wheat falling to the ground.

His death was a seed of thought in young Saul's mind.

Stephen bore many seeds through his death and the conversion of Paul (a.k.a. Saul). There are countless Christians because of Paul, countless Apostles to whom he wrote letters of encouragement.

Jesus was the mind of them all, through the Holy Spirit.

Now Peter, in his letter to those early Christians, who were facing all sorts of persecution, perhaps not all as bad as Stephen faced but persecution still the same, he encouraged them to "long for pure, spiritual milk, so that you may grow into salvation."

"So you may grow into salvation" means, "So Jesus will return to take you to the place prepared for you in Heaven," which comes by letting Jesus be you.

We are each a planned building, a church to God.

They have said, "The body is the temple to the soul," and it is ... as long as that building has "a cornerstone chosen and precious" ... Jesus.

Jesus said, "Believe in God, believe also in me."

Peter wrote, "Let yourselves be built into a spiritual house,

Easter Sermons: Fifth Sunday of Easter, Year A

to be a holy priesthood, to offer spiritual sacrifices acceptable to God through Jesus Christ."

You must let Jesus be you.

Once you were nothing (just as the children of Israel once were not a people).

But, with Jesus as you, you are God's choice (just as the children of Israel were chosen by God).

Once you had not received mercy (because you rejected the cornerstone and were more important than anyone else).

Now you can receive the Spirit along with the mercy of salvation (as did the disciples when they became Apostles in Christ).

Jesus said, "The one who believes in me will also do the works that I do and, in fact, will do greater works than these."

"Look! I see the heavens opened and the Son of Man at the right hand of God!"

Be that right hand of Christ.

Amen

# SIXTH SUNDAY OF EASTER

# YEAR A

**Relevant readings:**
Acts 17:22-31
Psalm 66:8-20
1 Peter 3:13-22
John 14:15-21

## Finding "Consummate Love" through Christ

We have reached the sixth Sunday of Easter, meaning we are 42 days into the counting of the 50 – to Pentecost, the fiftieth day.

We have another week with the risen Lord. We still have

time to spend in his physical presence, time learning from him, before he ascends to Heaven. We have more time to learn, until he leaves us next Saturday. The hope is he leaves us prepared to welcome him back into this world as ourselves.

Today's lessons tell us the next step of this preparedness, when Peter encouraged believers to remember, "In your **hearts sanctify** Christ as Lord."

We make Christ **holy** through our **hearts**, by love and acceptance. And, from that, Peter said we "do not fear what they fear, [we] are not intimidated" by threats of persecution. We enter a holy relationship with the Lord through love, as which point fear disappears.

We read how John recalled Jesus saying, "If you **love** me, you will keep my commandments." **Love** is the key to living up to our "bargain" with the LORD, to being more than a disciple. Love is the key to becoming an Apostle.

Now John remembered teachings that Jesus gave during the Passover Seder evening, where the ritual calls for each participant to drink as much wine as one can, all while discussing holy matters. One learns from the father (or each family head) until passing out drunk and tired.

You will notice that none of the other Gospels include these statements by Jesus. Matthew and Mark were probably two sheets to the wind by that time, so we can excuse them for not remembering and writing about what John recalled.

Keeping that dulled state of alertness in mind, it makes more sense when Jesus said, "In a little while the world will no longer see me, but you will see me; because I live, you will also live. On that day you will know that I am in my Father, and you in me, and I in you." That was as confusing to his drunken disciples as it is to most of us here today.

"Huh?" I imagine some of the disciples must have said. At least, those who routinely heard scripture discussed and (without the influence of wine) found everything about religious discussions worth arguing about. Most today think such discussions are best not heard, lest friends be lost.

If you recall the Gospel reading last week, Jesus told the disciples he was going to his Father's place to prepare a home for them. Thomas and Philip struggled to comprehend that statement. So, you can imagine how difficult it was for them to follow this.

John Lennon made more sense when he wrote, "I am he as you are he as you are me, and we are all together" ... "coo coo coo choo."

Having the benefit of two thousand years of Christianity, and having others before us explain the meaning of words to us, we become more sober, if not brighter than were the disciples. We are not drunk on wine. Our heads are clear, and we are well rested.

As adult Christians who study Scripture, who hear the Scriptures read to them in church and who hear sermons preached about those Scriptures ... time and time again ... we think can more easily grasp what Jesus said that Passover evening.

For those newcomers and young adults here among us, let

me say that Jesus was referring to what the Church calls the Trinity.

"I am in my **Father**" means **GOD the FATHER**.

"And you in **me**" means the **HOLY SPIRIT**.

"And I in **you**" means the **JESUS the SON**.

We all know that, so that is not the topic of discussion today. As much as we need to understand how we connect those three points, resulting in the perfection of us being filled with the Holy Spirit, I just wanted to remind everyone of that meaning.

Remember, this is the sixth week of seven, so we need to begin realizing how we actually have to **do** something to make this "training season" (Easter) special.

What the key focus then turns back to is **love**. "If you **love** Jesus, you will keep his commandments."

This is where we lose focus and become like Thomas and Philip. "Uh, which commandments? Not the 'sell everything you have, give to the poor, and follow me' commandment, right?"

We hear such a common word as "**love**" and we become like Thomas, saying, "Lord, we don't know where you are going with "**love**," so how can we know if we are correctly loving you?" We become like Philip and say, "Lord, show us what you mean by **love** and that will be enough for us."

This brings to mind a psychologist named Robert Sternberg. I learned about his theory in school. Sternberg came up with a view on love that can be looked up on Wikipedia, under "Triangular Theory of Love."

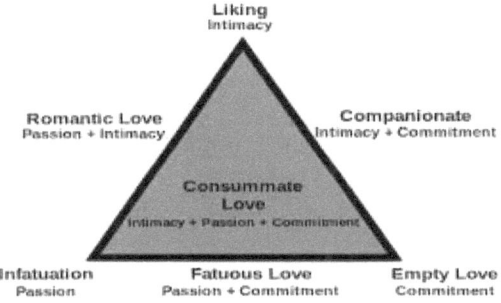

Rafy - Triangular_Theory_of_Love

Since we do not have a screen and overhead projector, imagine (or draw on the back of the bulletin) a triangle.

On a triangle there are three points, all of which represent different levels or aspects of **LOVE**.

At the top point is **INTIMACY**, which is a form of love that Sternberg called "Liking."

At the base of the triangle, on the left point is **INFATUATION**, or Passion.

At the base, on the right point is **EMPTY LOVE**, or Commitment.

Now in this theory of Sternberg's there is no question that the three points are identified as three recognized states of **LOVE**. However, because "Liking," "Passion," and "Commitment" are so different, we can see how – by Jesus simply saying, "If you **love** me" – this can be confusing.

Sternberg theorized that we often tie two of the points together, and we often tend to build relationships of merit from only two points, more than hitting the "trifecta" by connecting all three dots.

Relationships built from only one aspect of love struggle to be lasting. Many relationships fail to make that "Trinity" connection, where all three points make contact, igniting what Sternberg saw as "seven different kinds of love experiences."

For all three points to reflect a **LOVE** relationship, Sternberg called that Consummate Love.

When Jesus said to his disciples, "**Love** me," he wanted more than just to be "BFF's." He wanted **total love** to be the result.

As Christians, since Jesus is no longer physically with us, that makes a relationship harder to "consummate." We may only "**love**" Jesus from one point. According to what Jesus said – "**Love** me" – we think can meet the basic requirement by only having "Empty Love."

Now, let me explain what Sternberg meant by "Empty Love."

He defined it as being, "Characterized by commitment without intimacy or passion." A stronger love may deteriorate into empty love. In an arranged marriage, the spouses' relationship may begin as empty love and develop into another form, indicating "how empty love need not be the terminal state of a long-term relationship ... [but] the beginning rather than the end."

As life-long Christians, it is not uncommon to realize how we truthfully can say, "I love Jesus," but we say it knowing the words are without passion or intimacy.

We are committed to Christ. We are in a relationship of love with Jesus ... but it is Empty Love.

Sternberg called a two-pointed love, of Liking and Commitment, "COMPANIONATE LOVE." We are **committed friends** of Jesus ... which is exactly the same relationship each of the disciples had with Jesus.

One-pointed Empty Love and two-pointed Companionate Love are much better than not knowing Christ at all, or not having any relationship with him in any manner of love.

With Empty Love and Companionate Love there is the potential ... the promise for more.

That is what the Easter season of weeks is about.

As children, born into baptism and a marriage with Christ, that arrangement needs to grow into a close and personal relationship, more than one that has been arranged by our parents.

We need to change a one-pointed and/or two-pointed love into one that is three-dimensional – Consummate Love.

That requires the Holy Spirit, which is (as Jesus said) attracted by love.

Sternberg said that Consummate Love represents the "perfect couple." It is a relationship full of delight, one which is longer lasting and more fulfilling. However, he cautioned that "maintaining consummate love may be harder than achieving it." He warned, "Without **expression** even the greatest of loves can die."

This, of course was focusing on sexual relationships between human beings. A marriage bonded by the Holy Spirit taps into an eternal source of love; but the warning of Sternberg still applies. We must **express** love to maintain our marriage with God, which begets us the Christ.

When we see a triangle icon representing LOVE, where three points connect through three sides, we can also see the triangle icon of the Trinity.

It has been said that a triangle is the strongest shape, as each side supports the other two. We like that strength symbolized in the Trinity.

At the top point is the Father.

At the right side base point is the Son, who is Jesus.

At the left side base is the Holy Spirit, who is this mysterious entity that confuses many Christians.

My brother-in-law, an Episcopalian on paper, has admitted he has deep reservations about belief in this concept of a Trinity. He believes in God. He believes in Jesus as the Son of God. But, in a third being with the Father and the Son, he struggles to grasp that.

In a way, he would also struggle with the concept of CONSUMMATE LOVE. He believes in himself as the husband and father. He believes in his wife as his companion for life and the mother of his two sons. BUT ... I think he is confused about how his marriage can be a forty-year love affair, filled with the passion and infatuation of the unknown. I think he sees that Trinity as simply a matter of will power, not the hand of God, because connection just two points can make a thick, solid, unbreakable line of love.

This confusion in the "shape" of love, I believe, is assisted by focusing on that imagery of a triangle.

There are only two entities in play: the Father – God, who rules from the Spiritual realm; and the Son – Jesus the man, who connected to God in the Physical realm.

The point where the Spiritual joins with the Physical is then where the Holy Spirit resides. It is when God's Spiritual essence links with the Son's physical presence, making (and borrowing from the movie *Farris Beuller's Day Off*) ... Jesus "One Righteous Dude."

The symbol for that is not a triangle, but a cross.

Rose Cross by RootofAllLife

# Easter Sermons: Sixth Sunday of Easter, Year A

One plus One equals Three. It is new math at work.

We only see two, but the intersection where both are joined as a third explains how seeing the Holy Spirit is difficult. By seeing three separate points, it is hard to imagine how all can come together as One.

That center point is then representative of where the heart lies. Thus, **love** is the key to making this union, as the heart is where love resides.

Empty Love is Commitment, which is more of a mental state than it is heart-centered. We are committed to being Christian in mind, even if not in actions.

Companionate Love is again more of a mental state, where we like the idea of Jesus, and we think we are special because Jesus forgives us for all the sins we do, and we think it is the right thing to commit to Jesus …

But we still have not fully opened up our hearts and welcomed Jesus to come in.

Jesus comes in through the Holy Spirit.

Then, once welcomed in, the Holy Spirit becomes God in **Us**. Then, **we** each become the **Son**, through the Mind of Christ. God comes into us because we **love** Jesus so much. Because we can allow a Consummate Love for Jesus to take hold, we can become like Jesus. We can become a glory to the Father, through the Holy Spirit, as the Son reincarnated.

Jesus said, "Because I live, you also will live." Together we live, each of us with Christ.

Jesus said, "On that day," – when we each open our hearts and **love** Jesus, so we can receive the Spirit – "you will know that Jesus is in his Father." Your mind will expand to see the world through the eyes of God, through the mind of Christ, in the heart of you.

You will know that we are in Jesus. We will look like us to our friends, as outwardly nothing physically will have changed; but, inwardly and Spiritually we know we have changed into Jesus. We are no longer wandering lost, easily distracted by the bells and whistles of the material realm. The Holy Spirit becomes our focus, our source to boundless **love**.

You will know that Jesus is in you, because you will be holy. You will feel the joy of Christ in your heart and be overwhelmed by the presence of God with your soul. You will know Jesus on an intimate level. You will know the passion of Jesus. Your commitment to Jesus will be cemented forever.

Receive the Spirit by learning the lesson of God's CONSUMMATE **LOVE**.

Amen

ns: Sixth Sunday of Easter, Year A

# SEVENTH SUNDAY OF EASTER

# YEAR A

**Relevant readings:**
Acts 1:6-14
Psalm 68:1-10 and
Psalm 68:32-35
1 Peter 4:12-14 and
1 Peter 5:6-11
John 17:1-11

## On the verge of being lean, mean, fighting for Christ machines

We are now at the seventh Sunday of the Easter season – the Counting of the Omer, heading to the Festival of Weeks (*Shavout*).

# Easter Sermons: Seventh Sunday of Easter, Year A

In the Jewish count, the 50th day is tomorrow. In our Christian numbering system, next Sunday is our recognition of Pentecost (the 50th day).

So, what does it all mean?

<Pause>

Over the past six Sundays we have learned that a "training period" is required ... between gaining faith and having that faith become elevated by the Holy Spirit.

If you have ever been in the military, or seen a military movie or television show that focuses on Basic Training, you know that is a time of hard work and preparation.

Being filled with the Holy Spirit is pretty much like becoming a trained soldier; but it is like everything, really ... you have to drill until you automatically react. If you are ever going to be good at something, then you have to work hard at making that happen.

If you want to be a carpenter or woodworker, then you have to learn to use the proper tools. You have to gather machines and supplies. You have to set up a workshop. You have to draw plans; and you have to actually work to build something that passes inspection and gains praise.

If you want to be a school teacher, then you have to go to school ... a lot. If you want to be a lawyer, then you have to study the law ... also a lot. If you want to be an artist or musician, you have to learn an instrument or craft and practice, practice, practice.

Everything requires practice, practice, practice.

Practice makes perfect. It is a desire to master what you want to do that motivates one from within to do what all is physically demanded. The inner drive spurs the outer manifestation.

You can dream great dreams; but great dreams do not become reality unless you **ACT**.

It is easiest to **ACT** when we get to **DO** something we enjoy doing, something that brings satisfaction and a feeling of accomplishment.

Today is the seventh week that we have had lessons telling us that the time is coming when we will be required to **ACT**.

We read from the Book of the **ACTS** of the Apostles during this period.

In the Church calendar, last Thursday was Ascension Day ... but ... Christ did not ascend on a Thursday. Ordinary people do things on Thursday. Holy people do holy things on holy days. The Sabbath is the Lord's Day and must be kept holy. Jesus ascended on a *Shabbat* ... not a Thursday.

We see this holy symbolism of holy days in Scripture ... if we know how to look for it.

Jesus presided over the Last Supper as a Jewish *Shabbat* turned into the first day of the Passover week (Sunday, or *yom rishon*). Jesus was raised from death on a Jewish

## Easter Sermons: Seventh Sunday of Easter, Year A

*Shabbat*, eight days after the Passover week began, also on a Sabbath. He was discovered not in his tomb on Sunday, the first day of the week.

For six weeks after the events of Easter Sunday, the Risen Christ presided over Basic Training, where the disciples were whipped into shape, becoming Apostles.

On the forty-ninth day (seven weeks after the Seder meal that bridged between the *yom shabbat* and *yom rishon*) Christ Ascended to Heaven. That occurrence took place on a Jewish *Shabbat*, a holy day, the day of the Lord.

God is the one controlling all this ... I hope you can understand that. There is no randomness to anything relative to Jesus Christ. Everything has meaning.

This, of course, means the Pentecost was on a Sunday ... the Fiftieth day .. the day after Jesus left his troops prepared to take over for him.

Today, we hear the conversation that took place between Jesus and God, as John watched and listened below. John listened as Jesus was dying on the cross before him.

Jesus was seeing the future when he said, "And now I am no longer in the world, but they are in the world, and I am coming to you, Holy Father, protect them in your name that you have given me, so that they may be one, as we are one."

We are in the world

*<knock loudly on podium>*

… hear that? It is the sound of matter, not ether.

We need protection, which comes from the title given Jesus. In Greek, that title is "*Christos*" or "Christ," which means "Anointed." The Hebrew equivalent word is "*mashiach*," which we capitalize as "Messiah." Both words mean "Anointed." Anointment is an ACT of the Father to His Son; but God the Father has the right and the means to "Anoint" whoever He deems fit to wear that title.

In order to truly be Christians, we must <u>first</u> believe in Jesus as Christ, the Messiah, our Savior, Redeemer, Champion and Protector.

Jesus prayed, "So that they **MAY** be one, as we are one."

In the English language, the word "may" is an auxiliary verb, in the future conditional tense, where "would + may = might."

It is a hopeful statement, about what **MAY** occur after Jesus' death, resurrection, and ascension; but it is a "woulda, coulda, shoulda" condition. There is no guarantee.

The word "may" stems from the infinitive verb, "to be able." It's use as "may" means conditions exist that enable us to be one with God and Christ, as God and Christ are one, as Jesus and God were one; but that condition requires a future action, based on the recognition of what one is **ABLE** to achieve.

We **MAY** be one with God if we have faith that Christ will Advocate on our behalf, so God will send into us His Holy

Easter Sermons: Seventh Sunday of Easter, Year A

Spirit.

That is what we celebrate about the Pentecost (the Fiftieth day).

That is why we spend seven weeks drilling about what the Easter season means, which makes us **ABLE** to be one with God. We need to be **ABLE** to be transformed from disciples into Apostles. We must strive to be **ABLE** to morph from recruits to soldiers.

In the reading from the Book of the Acts of the Apostles today, we imagine the form of Jesus rising upward, towards Heaven, while all his disciples watched.

They were moved by the vision. The thought of themselves going to the heavenly kingdom someday mesmerized them. They were dreaming, while still gazing at blue sky. Jesus was already "out of their sight" by then.

Suddenly, two men in white robes got their attention and snapped them back to reality.

"What's going on guys?" they asked. "Don't you know it is time to get to work, and stop doing more than dreaming?"

When we read, "Then they returned to Jerusalem from the mount called Olivet," that says the Ascension occurred near the same place where Jesus prayed, at Gethsemane.

We then read that "the mount called Olivet" is "a Sabbath day's journey away" from Jerusalem. That means Passover week began on a Jewish *Shabbat*, Jesus rose from death on a Jewish *Shabbat*, and the Ascension was likewise on a Jewish *Shabbat*, because they had travelled as far as was allowed on that holy day (roughly half a mile outside the city).

In Acts 1:6, we find that the disciples are now called "apostles." They have changed titles, just as the man named Jesus was given the title Christ, by God, on the day he was born as a marriage of the flesh and soul with God, via the Holy Spirit. The disciples had completed Basic Training and passed inspection, in the eyes of God and Christ. They have grown into lean, mean, fighting machines … in a good sense.

Graduation would come the next day, Pentecost Sunday.

The new apostles got down to the business at hand … deciding who was going to replace Judas on the executive board.

While eleven is a special number, twelve is a better "round number" with its own special meaning.

Still, the work of Apostles requires action. Thus, we read that "All these ["board members"] were constantly devoting themselves to prayer." Prayer is an action.

Still, because we see that those who were the other followers of Jesus, believers in him as the Christ, they too were elevated as Apostles, while being women and relatives. They too were constantly devoted to prayer.

The reason one needs to be drilled and trained, made to hurt and ache, is so the body steadily develops the necessary muscles that allows one to morph into a state of readiness. Training is essential if one is to meet the challenge of hard work that an Apostle must withstand.

Peter wrote, in his first letter, words of encouragement for the growing numbers of Apostles. He expressed, as would have Jesus, a need to withstand pain and suffering.

He wrote about "the fiery ordeal that is taking place among you," which says they were under a lot of heat. There is still a "fiery ordeal taking place," which we need to face.

Peter advised the followers of Jesus to withstand persecution by those who "reviled (them) for the name of Christ." Jesus was reviled because he had the title as the "Anointed" one. Peter wrote as one likewise "Anointed," who knew the persecution that comes to all who will be Jesus reborn. His letter was sent to others also so "Anointed."

Peter wrote, "Cast all your anxiety on him … discipline yourselves, keep alert … (be) steadfast in your faith." Jesus told his Father, "the spirit is willing, but the flesh is weak." Jesus cast his own anxieties onto the Christ title God had bestowed upon him.

The world is still filled with those who revile people who look nothing like Jesus, but are disciplined via the Christ. Unfortunately, fewer these days know how to be "Anointed." Today, anxiety is more likely treated with drugs, than with faith in God's Christ.

Peter, in his letter, then admitted there would be suffering, but that was what they were trained **TO BE ABLE** to resist. He wrote, "After you have suffered for a little while, the God of all grace, who called you to his eternal glory in Christ, will himself restore, support, strengthen, and establish you." The Holy Spirit makes a disciple **ABLE** as an Apostle.

That says you are made **ABLE** because of God, and His Holy Spirit. You cannot withstand all the pain and suffering that disciples attract, without that aid. Without graduating from Christ's Basic Training, you are not strong enough.

Remember, it was Peter's faith that Jesus questioned. Peter, the "pet name" given by Jesus to Simon bar Jonah, a name that means "Rock," was not strong enough to live up to that material world title, without the Holy Spirit.

As a lowly disciple, Peter denied Jesus three times before the cock crowed. It was Peter who struck out at Gethsemane, in fear of losing Jesus. He cut the ear off a guard coming to take Jesus away.

It was Peter who wanted so much to walk on water, only to sink like a stone, because he lacked enough faith to be without fear.

Fear is what keeps one from gaining the strength of the Holy Spirit.

Fear comes from allowing yourself to hear the roaring lion in your adversary, the devil, who prowls around looking for weak disciples to devour. Fear makes you run and hide, just as did the disciples after the Romans (inspired by the Jews) nailed Jesus to a tree.

Easter Sermons: Seventh Sunday of Easter, Year A

Fear keeps you going from one Easter season to another Easter season, still as disciples … still as sheep standing comfortably in the sheepfold, side-by-side with others just like you, feeling safety in numbers … free from the pains and sufferings the shepherding Apostles endure.

**May** you be one with God, through faith in Christ.

Amen

# PENTECOST SUNDAY

# YEAR A

**Relevant readings:**
Acts 2:1-21 or
Numbers 11:24-30
Psalm 104:25-37
1 Corinthians 12:3-13
or Acts 2:1-21
John 20:19-23 or
John 7:37-39

## The fiftieth day is not ordinary unless you passed the exam

I wish we had programmed the organ to play Pomp and Circumstance, because today is graduation day. [The organ

# Easter Sermons: Pentecost Sunday, Year A

at St. Stephen's was programmable, as no one there could play the organ.]

The high schools in Marion County ended May 23, and the seniors attended graduation ceremonies then.

The Summer Vacation period for school children is already underway.

However, for us adult Episcopalians, according to our liturgical calendar, today we should honor a different class of graduates; and for them there is no vacation that kicks off that recognition.

Today is Pentecost Sunday. Tomorrow, although we Episcopalians do not recognize it, is Whit Monday ("Whit" is Old English for "White"). Tomorrow is also known as Pentecost Monday or the Monday of the Holy Spirit.

Whatever you call tomorrow, Monday begins the liturgical period called "Ordinary Time."

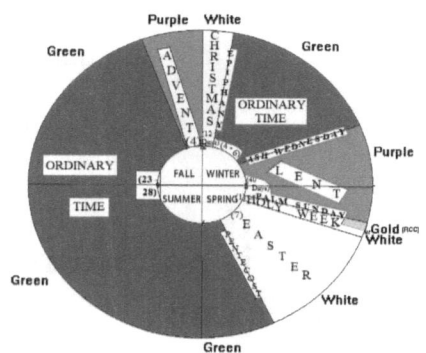

Ordinary Time covers the period from Pentecost Monday until the First Sunday of Advent.

Robert Tippett

Raise your hands if you understand why we call that Ordinary Time.

If everyone raises your hand, then we will have 5 minutes of silence. Otherwise, I will explain the meaning to those who do not know.

<pause - *look for hands raised*>

You may have met David Johnson before. He was here when Lyn was ordained, last December. He holds the title of Mississippi Diocese Canon to the Ordinary.

As a Canon to the Ordinary, "David Johnson provides counsel to the Diocesan bishop," where Bishop Gray is the Ordinary officer of the Church in our state of Mississippi.

With the bishop, the Canon oversees the ordination process, including the one-year program of "ordinands training." An "ordinand" is "a candidate for ordination."

Thus, when we reach the longest liturgical season of the year, Ordinary Time, that denotes a time for the Ordained. It is when those who are Ordained have the power of bishops, to spend the majority of a year ministering to the people.

Because we all have spent the last seven weeks being trained, through the inspiration of the readings in the Easter Weeks ... the Christian version of the Counting of the Omer ... we have reached the Day of Graduation ... Pentecost Sunday. A new class of Ordinands should be presented for all to appreciate.

## Easter Sermons: Pentecost Sunday, Year A

We should have new Apostles coming forward now, to receive certificates of ordination, before they would be sent out tomorrow ... one White Monday, denoting that their sins have been erased and their hearts are pure, ceremoniously dressed in white robes ... to go out into the world and spread the Gospel to those not yet filled with the Holy Spirit.

Still, while graduates go forth during Ordinary Time, as Ordained with the Holy Spirit, they begin a life where being filled with the Holy Spirit becomes "ordinary" to them.

Being filled with the Holy Spirit means forever onward facing whatever the world brings as a challenge to one's faith, as "usual or normal condition or course of events." (A definition of "ordinary.")

The talents of the Ordained, or their gifts of the Holy Spirit, are classified as, "Of common or established types." To them, the Holy Spirit is, "Commonplace." More definitions of the word "ordinary."

Raise your hand if you graduated from high school so long ago that it feels like you always had that knowledge.

<pause - *look at hands*>

Raise your hands if you were Ordained on a Pentecost past, or your own personal day with God and Christ, and that day was so long ago that being filled with the Holy Spirit seems commonplace to you now.

<pause - *look at hands*>

There is nothing "ordinary" about the Holy Spirit, and while its early spread gave rise to the world's greatest religion - Christianity - after many centuries less and less Ordinations by the Holy Spirit are taking place, making Christians more and more "ordinary."

Today, we read again in the Book of Acts, of the Day of Pentecost, when the Apostles first were filled with the Holy Spirit.

The words say it came upon them suddenly, accompanied by a sound that is described as being "like the rush of a violent wind."

Have you ever watched the news on television, where a reporter asked someone who survived a tornado to explain the ordeal? I know Jeff Foxworthy has a joke about being a redneck, if you have ever been seen on the news saying, "It sounded like a freight train," before your trailer park was destroyed.

A tornado has a sound "like the rush of a violent wind." Raise your hand if you have heard a tornado.

<pause - *look at hands*>

The point is there was a clearly recognizable sound that accompanied that presence in the house of the Apostles.

That says, "If you have been filled with the Holy Spirit, then you don't have to think about it." You know immediately, not, "maybe I was or maybe I wasn't."

## Easter Sermons: Pentecost Sunday, Year A

It overcomes you so suddenly that you are strongly impacted. That presence causes a difference to come within you, so strongly you never forget when that happened.

Of course when that happened to the Apostles (who were no longer disciples because of their Graduation), all the people who heard them speaking in foreign tongues thought about what they were hearing. They knew with their minds that simple country folk could not know the languages of places those rubes had never been. The brains of the pilgrims told them that the Apostles must just drunk on new wine.

Brains think "it sounded like a freight train," because nobody is afraid of freight trains. They stay safely on tracks, but they make noises that can be heard a long way off. The pilgrims, at first, though the noises made by the apostles were just loud noises in the distance.

You know how it is when you hear a drunk. People in that state of being can sometimes take chances that they never would when sober. Sometimes, inexplicably, drunk people can do some amazing things ... simply by accident; the luck of the draw.

The visiting pilgrims thought the Apostles were just babbling, not knowing what they were saying, only by some crazy chance did the noises the apostles were making seem to be languages the foreigners understood. Just like a drunk person might slip and begin to fall, but instead they do some Olympic gymnast move and it looks like they planned to do that ... the minds of the pilgrims deduced, "It must be that."

People who have not been filled with the Holy Spirit like to explain away those who are so filled with an ability to do extraordinary things, out of the blue. It is commonplace to not give credit to those who do amazing things without explanation. If in doubt ... all is ordinary.

Of course, we sip wine at the altar because Jesus passed around the cup of wine, saying, "This is the blood of the New Covenant. Whenever you drink this, remember me."

That, of course, does not mean if you drink a whole bottle of wine and remember Jesus, then you will be filled with the Holy Spirit. Drunk from the spirits of alcohol, yes; but not close to holiness.

In Paul's letter to the Corinthians, he made a very important statement, one which might be overlooked or misunderstood.

He said, "No one can say, "Jesus is Lord" except by the Holy Spirit."

That does **not** mean, "If you say, "Jesus is Lord," then you are filled with the Holy Spirit."

It says, "By the power of the Holy Spirit within him, Jesus (the man) was God incarnate." You must see how Jesus acted in each of the ways Paul then listed, each of which demonstrates the Holy Spirit was in Jesus. You must recognize the Holy Spirit, in order for one to say, "Jesus is Lord."

Because Jesus displayed those gifts of the Holy Spirit, so too will any and all others who believe in Christ and God, and who enrol into that "school" of thought ... becoming disciples ... then graduating, as Apostles, knowingly filled with the Holy Spirit. Those are the ones Ordained to spread that to others, just as Jesus spread it to them.

When you realize this, you can see how the ways of the Jews at the time of Christ were to be followers. They depended on leaders; content that they (for the most part) would never achieve a leadership role of religious importance.

That was the "ordinary" way for them to be. They were conditioned to be sheep, in need of a shepherd to follow.

The Jews followed either the Pharisees or the Sadducees (the main political sects of the day), who were thereby ordained by the scribes (the seminary professors of the day) and anointed by the Temple's High Priest. "Go out and practice law," was their graduation day encouragement. Those rulers of the Jews were disciples of Judaism, with none trained to receive the Holy Spirit.

Although many of those rulers recognized they needed to be more, to do more, they just learned how to get by on their wiles, complaining to God and their leaders (under their breath). Meanwhile, all the normal Jews, those who believed being one of God's chosen people **must** mean more than memorizing laws they could never live up to, they wanted to be taught what God wants from them.

Peter stood up before the crown in Jerusalem for the Festival of Weeks (*Shavuot*), begun on the Fiftieth day (Pentecost), proclaiming, "People in Jerusalem, we are not drunk!"

Peter said, "We are like those Joel prophesied would come, 'In the last days.'"

The last days Joel wrote of were not some distant times of our future, which (by then) were certainly their times. Instead, Joel wrote of the end of Judaism as being the way to heaven.

Jews believed they were the chosen people of God, and merely by being Jewish disciples of the One God they would be rewarded with Heaven (a birthright). They never imagined they should, could, or would ever graduate to the level of priests or rabbis, without being born into that private clique.

That system would begin to come to an end when Galileans spoke fluently in foreign languages, speaking with tongues set on fire by the Holy Spirit ... without being drunk. Those were the last days, when "Sons and daughters would prophesy, old men would have dreams, and young men would have visions."

Think about that: Boys and girls - children - would understand the Word of God; the old would be able to prophesy through dreams of wisdom that they would share; and the rest of mature adults of Judaic faith would be able to see the meaning and truth written into the scrolls they read every Saturday.

A new religion was marked by those who had the Holy Spirit, and could "utter wisdom and knowledge" that was beyond one's educational level. It foretold of a time when believers would "show profound levels of faith," stronger than the mere memorization of written text. It prophesied of times that would "heal" those in need and produce "miracles" witnessed by many. It meant a time coming when it was Ordinary to "prophesy" and "interpret prophecy," "understand foreign languages," and "discern spirits" that were the inner motivations and influences within others.

Jesus Christ marked the end of the old ways, the ways of devotion through following. His return into the first graduating class of those who would bear his title, as "Christians," meant the beginning of a new way, a way of devotion by acting from complete faith, **FILLED WITH THE HOLY SPIRIT**.

That was Joel's prophecy, remembered by Simon-Peter. It is a truth that existed for Jesus and the Apostles then; but it is also an eternal prophecy of truth, which spoke for all the patriarchs and prophets of old, as well as all the Saints born throughout the age of Christianity.

Each of the Apostles had at least one of those gifts, with some possessing more than one. They became arms of God, just as the physical body of Jesus had been. They became the "members" of the "body of Christ," through being filled with the same powers of God that Jesus had been given.

Once you graduate as an Ordained Apostle, then you are "renewed by the Spirit," "so you renew the face of the earth."

Your hearts grow ten times larger, as did the Grinch's. It becomes so large that "rivers of living water" flow from you, for others who thirst to drink.

Peace overcomes you, so there is no fear of anyone or anything, other than God.

> "Ye though I walk through the shadow of the valley of death I shall fear no evil."

Peace be with you, when you are filled with the Holy Spirit.

Jesus said to his disciples, when they feared for their mortal lives, "Peace be with you. As the Father has sent me, so I send you."

So the Father sent Jesus with the Holy Spirit, so too will Jesus send you with the Holy Spirit.

"Receive the Holy Spirit," because God forgives the sins of any who accept the breath of Christ into their hearts. For those who hold onto to their material addictions and the sins of sacrifice made for meaningless things in this physical realm, you can retain those things … until death do you part.

You can choose eternal life, or you can choose death. The last days of being a sheep, led by wolves in sheep's clothing have come. There are lost sheep to gather, and the world needs some Good Shepherds.

When will you graduate from disciple to Apostle, from sheep to Shepherd? When will you be prepared to be ordained by the Holy Spirit?

Amen

# Easter Sermons: Pentecost Sunday, Year A

# EASTER SERMONS

# YEAR B

# EASTER SUNDAY

# YEAR B

**Relevant readings:**
Acts 10:34-43 or
Isaiah 25:6-9
Psalm 118:1-2 & 14-24
1 Corinthians 15:1-11 or
Acts 10:34-43
John 20:1-18 or
Mark 16:1-8

## Why did Jesus appear in an unrecognizable form?

Christ is risen!

# Easter Sermons: Easter Sunday, Year B

*The Lord is risen indeed!*

Alleluia!

Last week I told you the story ends well and not to stay focused on the death of Jesus. Happy day! Jesus is no longer dead! Long live the King!

You have to see that the Resurrection of Jesus was just as he told the disciples before his arrest, when Greek Jews asked to come and see him.

He said, "Very truly I tell you, unless a kernel of wheat falls to the ground and dies, it remains only a single seed. But if it dies, it produces many seeds."

Are there any farmers here today?

<look for raised hands>

The Passion of the Christ was – in essence – the sowing of a very important seed in the earth.

It was sown into fertile ground, which Jesus had prepared and tilled for three years.

Once the seeds are sown into the fields, the farmers have to be patient, while the "seed dies," before the first shoots appear … then more patient until the fruits of their labors appear as intended … and still more patience until the harvest time has come.

Jesus had to die so a strong root could take firm hold in the soil of Israel, before shooting towards the light, breaking open the ground, rising towards the sky.

Today, we see how our patience through Holy Week has paid off. Jesus has broken through the covering of earth and risen.

"Why were you weeping? Who were you looking for? A mortal son of man, unjustly tried, convicted, and hung on a tree till death? Or, the Son of God?"

In John's Gospel, where Mary Magdalene has come to see the tomb is opened and her lord is not there, John told of a conversation between the Spirit of Jesus and Mary.

Mary had only known Jesus as a man ... a seed, not as a new shoot of vine ... a new growth looking nothing like before. So, she did not recognize her lord until she heard his voice.

Jesus said to Mary, "Do not hold onto me, because I have not yet ascended to the Father."

Jesus was freshly risen, and still tender. A farmer does not go out into the fields and touch each new growth, as they all need time to gain more strength.

Still, the meaning of what Jesus said to Mary was meant to tell her not to think physical Jesus is back to stay. She did not yet understand that Jesus had not resurrected like Lazarus had been, with Lazarus still living and (according to legend) would live for decades more. Jesus told Mary the returned man she knew before his death would not be around very long. He would ascend to the Father in forty-two days.

Jesus was in a state of transformation, much like the appearance of Moses and Elijah had appeared with Jesus on the high mountain. We call that the Transfiguration, but it foretold of Jesus transforming to be much more than any one man could be. Jesus could not be held onto because he was the growth of God's vine, from which would come so many more. He could not he held onto as an individual.

He told her, "Do not hold onto the thought of me as one human body of flesh."

A seed is primarily an embryo inside a seed covering or shell. Likewise, a soul is covered by flesh. The two are one, from birth to death.

In order for a soul to ascend into heaven, the body has to die ... just as the seed coat of a seed must be shed, so the embryo can transform into a greater being.

When you see this imagery of Jesus planted in the tomb, you can see the seed covering left behind was his shroud – the *tahrihim*– and his face covering – the *soudarion*.

You can see why John said Jesus appeared as the gardener, because a gardener is one who cultivates plants, making them grow. We know the tomb of Joseph of Arimathea was in a place with a garden, since John (19:41) stated as much:

> "Now in the place where he was crucified there was a garden, and in the garden a new tomb in which no one had yet been laid."

Still, there is more than "just the facts ma'am" that needs to

Robert Tippett

be seen from this "gardener" assumption.

If you close your eyes and imagine, you might be able to see the unrecognizable body of the gardener, as seen by Mary and John, was in the form of one who had the soul of Jesus within ... as the one who once lived in human form in a great garden called Eden.

The Son of God ... in Hebrew he was called Adam ... meaning Man.

Jesus spoke to Mary as the Son of Adam ... the Son of Man ... in a voice Mary recognized as that of her Lord ... her *Rabbouni* ... the Son of God.

In that recognizable voice, while in an unrecognizable form, Jesus told Mary, "Go to my brothers and say to them, 'I am ascending to my Father and your Father, to my God and your God.'"

That command came from the vine that would bear living fruit. The "brothers" would assist in the production of that fruit ... and as the first fruits.

As the vine of Christ grew, his tendrils extended to grab hold of physical structures, in order to reach maturity and begin producing the fruit of the vine.

The young sprout that was Christ sought to adhere to the trellises that had been set into the vineyard, by Jesus. Those trellises were his disciples that he called his "brothers." They were all related by blood and marriage; but they were brothers as they too would all become the sons of God.

In Paul's first letter to the Corinthians, he outlined this vineyard that was designed and laid out by Jesus.

The first branches of the vine clung to the Cross (Stake-Pole-*Stauros*) that was the family of Jesus, who assisted him in his ministry, providing him with the necessary supplies and housing, while believing in his holiness.

Cephas (aka Cleopas or Clopas) was Jesus' uncle, married to Mary Salome, the sister-in-law of Mary, the mother of Jesus. Cephas and Mary were an unwritten part of the Christmas story, as Joseph was Cephas' brother. They were amazed by baby Jesus and had known him all his life. Now, Jesus appeared to Cleopas and Mary Salome on the road to Emmaus ... after he appeared as a gardener to Mary Magdalene ... more family who assisted Jesus the Rabbi.

No one recognized the resurrection of Jesus then. His aunt and uncle did not recognize him until "he took the bread and blessed and broke it and gave it to them." (Luke 24:30b) They too heard his voice and were made aware.

The second set of trellises the vine of Christ adhered to were the poles created by the disciples of Jesus, his group of students, which numbered "twelve." Others certainly assisted them and had seen the disciples with Jesus the man and the Rabbi. That number includes those who Jesus had healed, having touched them personally to their heart-centers. They were extended family members; but the "brothers" of Jesus were his direct family and aides.

In Paul's listing of Jesus' blessings by appearance, he then throws Christian scholars a statement that causes a question mark to appear over their heads. He did this by naming the third branch upon which the vine of Christ was strung, when he wrote, "Then [Jesus] appeared to more than five hundred brothers and sisters at one time."

No other New Testament author supports this claim directly. So scratch and offer theories that maybe Jesus encountered (over 40 days) 500 people in Galilee, while his Spirit was teaching his disciples. However, it is doubtful that anyone then would have known this person not looking like Jesus was Jesus **AND** that was not at one time.

This statement by Paul has to be understood as the power of God that was in Jesus. One did not come into close, personal contact with Jesus (as the stories in the Gospels tell) and have those who were touched not come away forever inspired. The leper who came back to thank Jesus, the Samaritan woman and her family members, the woman near Tyre and Sidon ... on and on they go ...they all saw the Jesus that had touched them **vividly**, while Jesus was appearing in unrecognizable form to his family. Jesus spoke to them as he had spoken to Paul and would speak to Peter near Rome. Jesus told those "five hundred brothers and sisters" in a divine state of being, spread over who knows how many miles of terrain, "at one time."

Following the appearance of the Spirit of Jesus to the disciples ... and after his Spirit spent forty days training them to become full-bodied, sweet-tasting grapes of Christ ... the next appearance of the Lord would be to the pilgrims of the following *Shavuot* – the Festival of Weeks, which began on the Day of Pentecost – the Fiftieth Day.

*Shavuot* represents the time when the Israelites harvested

the early wheat of spring ... which has to remind us of the "grain of wheat" that "bears much fruit," of which Jesus spoke.

Even if one assumes that Paul was numbering the crowd to which Peter spoke, saying that crowd numbered "five hundred brothers and sisters" who were gathered "at one time," one would doubt that Saul (then his name) would have been among first-hand witnesses to Peter and the other eleven speaking divinely. If he was writing from hearsay, then from those five hundred brothers and sister who hear the twelve at one time, then we must believe as we are told: that "about three thousand souls were baptized (with the Holy Spirit) that day." From twelve to five hundred to three thousand ... "Tag, you've got **IT** ... pass **it** on!"

The vine just shot out a cluster of grapes, all full of seeds.

The point of truth told by Paul then can only mean that Jesus appeared to that group of festival attendees in the body of Peter and the other eleven. Jesus appeared as all the Apostles that day. That is why the voice of Jesus told Mary Magdalene, "Do not hold onto me" in the flesh, because Jesus would hold onto Mary, through the Holy Spirit. Jesus would also become Mary, just as Jesus became Peter ... just as Jesus wants to become us.

From that dawning, we next read Paul stating the fourth branch was before the Cross of James (also called "the Just"), the brother of Jesus. James was the son of Mary, the wife of Joseph, thereby his son.

James was a half-brother to Jesus. They were raised together, in the same home. Thus, James did not see Jesus as more holy than he was. James was himself a rabbi, most likely an equal of a Pharisee, but with Essene upbringing.

James had said publicly that he would not eat of the bread of Jesus' last supper until he had seen for himself the risen brother he grew up with ... whom James knew was dead. James had not been shown Jesus had indeed resurrected.

The Spirit of Jesus appeared before his half-brother, blessed and broke new bread, Spiritual bread, which he gave to James to eat. James then became a Christian Jew, who used the Temple of Jerusalem as his synagogue to lead other Jews to believe their Messiah had truly come. You might recall that Stephen, the one who was filled with the Holy Spirit who became the first martyred Christian, was most probably given the Holy Spirit by James.

Thus, with many Stakes (Crosses) set into the garden of Christ, the good fruit of that vine became many apostles, which Paul said was the fifth branch of support.

This means that Jesus appeared to everyone who received the Spirit, through faith that Jesus was the Christ promised to the Jews, for the salvation of the world.

Every apostle looks different in body, but every apostle is Christ ... every apostle is a reborn Jesus ... just like the first unrecognizable Jesus appeared to Mary Magdalene. Jesus appears to them all ... and all heard his voice speaking to them.

Then, Paul told of the sixth branch, of which Paul himself was the foremost example.

# Easter Sermons: Easter Sunday, Year B

Paul, as Saul, was not a faithful Jew. He persecuted the Jews who followed Jesus. He stood by and watched over the coats of Jews who stoned Stephen to death. Saul probably smiled as that happened.

Saul did not believe there ever would be a Messiah. He saw the Roman Empire as eternal ... at least lasting through the rest of his natural life.

Saul was a Roman citizen - an association he held more dearly than his Jewish ancestry; and Saul did not seek the God of the Jews as a way to wealth and fame.

Then Jesus appeared to him, "the least of all the apostles," the one who then saw himself as "unfit to be called an apostle."

Saul became Paul. One whose name had meant "To ask" or "To question" ... as a doubter (Saul) ... that man became one who knew he was "Feeble, weak, and small" (Paul).

Paul had an epiphany when the Spirit of Jesus appeared to him. He realized no matter how much one gathers around one's self - things of this material world - one is never any larger than the minutest particle of dust that has been formed around an immeasurable soul.

Paul spoke for all of us here today, as none of us here are family of Jesus, nor are we disciples who broke bread with Jesus for three years of his time on earth. We are not relatives of James and Joseph, as partial relatives of Jesus' mother. Few (if any) of us here can lay claim to Jesus by possessing Jewish heritage in our blood.

We are not one of the five hundred Jews, most of whom (if not all) were still living when Paul wrote to the Corinthians. Today, all of them have long since died.

That leaves us to be (on the positive side) apostles, who have seen Jesus encounter us on our meaningless road of life, asking us, "Why do you refuse to receive the Spirit?"

If we did respond as did Saul-transformed-into-Paul, then that means others here should form a line to my right, waiting your turn to stand where I am now, and preach about things I have meant to say but didn't want to do all the talking.

That would be just as Peter did, standing before the crowd, inspiring the faithful with the voice of Jesus. We can do likewise and also bring others salvation, simply by welcoming Jesus into our hearts and minds, so he can do the talking, while we just move our lips.

Or … or … it leaves us to fall into the negative category of those like Saul … sinners who are too weak, feeble, or small to become apostles … refusing to own up to that character flaw.

Which "Mystery Date" are you, when God calls for a place to raise Jesus? Are you "a Stud" or are you "a Dud"?

Paul wrote to the Christians of Corinth to tell them, "The grace of God towards me has not been in vain."

That means, God did not bless Paul so Paul could be rich and famous … as one who would profit greatly from being the most published author in the New Testament. Paul was

# Easter Sermons: Easter Sunday, Year B

not an apostle who had Jesus appear to him for selfish – self-serving ... vain reasons.

Paul said, "On the contrary, I worked harder than any of the other apostles – though it was not I, but the grace of God with me."

In the beginning of this reading of Paul's letter, Paul wrote of those who held firmly to the message of Christ that Paul had sown in Corinth. He wrote to those who had heard the message and also saw Jesus within ...

with the caveat being the warning: "Unless you have come to believe in vain."

If you have come to say you believe in Jesus as Christ because it will (fill in the blank) **ME**, where the blank says, "save me," "make me rich," "forgive me so I can sin some more," "make me better than others," etcetera, etcetera, then you have come to believe in vain.

People put in a lot of hard work to make it seem that God has blessed them ... probably at least as much as Paul put into being an apostle of Christ ... and probably as much as Saul put into persecuting the church of God and its people.

After all ... we are all slaves on this bus ... no purple robes with ermine collars or tiaras for us, so hard work is what we know.

Paul saw Jesus and knew just how small and weak he was, despite all his efforts to the contrary.

We need to see ourselves in that same light.

That is because we are nothing more than what the "grace of God within" leads us to do for others. If we are going to work anyway, then let it be for the Lord, and not for selfish reasons.

We should be writing letters to others who need our support.

We should be preaching to the crowds … simply by opening our mouths and letting Jesus do the talking for us.

We need to stop being **us** and start being reborn as Jesus.

<pause>

On this Easter Sunday, when we so happily rejoice in the risen Lord, we need to realize Christ arose to return in everybody that holds a soul of God. The only thing stopping that is our refusal to be saved.

So, when Mary asked, "Where have you laid my Lord," we have to realize how she asked so that we can say, "Here Mary! He lies in me."

Amen

# Easter Sermons: Easter Sunday, Year B

# SECOND SUNDAY OF EASTER

# YEAR B

**Relevant readings:**
Acts 4:32-35
Psalm 133
1 John 1:1-2:2
John 20:19-31

## The measure of the Easter season

We have entered into the period known by the Jews (and Israelites) as the Counting of the Omer.

According to the Torah (Lev. 23:15), the Israelites (thus later the Jews) were obligated to count the days from Passover to *Shavuot*.

This period is known as the Counting of the Omer.

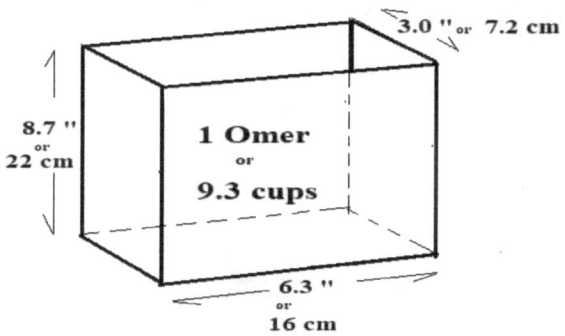

An "Omer" is a unit of measure. On the second day of Passover (in the days of the Temple) an omer of barley was cut down and brought to the Temple as an offering (called a "wave offering"). This grain offering was referred to as the Omer.

Every night, from the second night of Passover to the night before *Shavuot*, the Jews (then and today) recite a blessing and state the count of the omer in both weeks and days.

The counting is intended to remind them of the link between Passover, which commemorates the Exodus, and *Shavuot*, which commemorates the giving of the Torah. It reminds them that the redemption from slavery was not complete until they received the Torah.

The Passover Festival (during the times of the Temple of Jerusalem) lasted eight days, between 15 Nisan and 22 Nisan. The last Passover Jesus experienced, significantly began and ended on a sabbath day (*yom shabbat*).

As such, Jesus was raised on 22 Nisan, which was a *Shabbat*, with this discovered being early on Sunday morning, "the first day of the week." That Sabbath of Jesus' resurrection was the seventh day of the Counting of the Omer - Nisan 16 to Nisan 22.

The Counting of the Omer continues for 49 days, from the second day of Passover Week, until the day before the 50th day – Pentecost.

Pentecost thus begins *Shavuot*, which is called the Festival of Weeks ... the seven weeks of travel from bondage, until the delivery of the Law ... the First Covenant.

So, as Christians, it is important to see the correlation between the Jewish ritual of commitment and the Christian ritual of commitment, such that Christians have taken on the same commitments in order to become part of God's chosen people.

The fact that Jesus came to extend the priesthood to Gentiles, the people God chose first (the children of Israel) were themselves not trained in how specifically to serve only One God. They had to make an agreement that rules existed, in order to become God's priests - in training. This means us Gentiles - Christians - have to make the same agreements to accept the terms of the First Covenant, the same as did the Israelites.

Calling it the "Old Testament" does not make it become the "Obsolete Testament." The "New Testament" is an "Amended Testament," whereby the laws are written in the hearts of God's chosen people, rather than on a "new" set of stone tablets. The laws don't disappear in this transition

Easter Sermons: Second Sunday of Easter, Year B

from Old to New.

The "laws" include maintenance of the ritual recognitions of importance, where God has freed all of us here today, from slavery to sins - those that come from serving a multiple gods. This is our Passover - saved by the blood of Jesus, the sacrificial lamb.

God has given us the Law as His promise to protect those who agree to those terms, which becomes written on hearts that desire God and want to serve Him as did Jesus. This is our *Shavuot*.

God has also given us a command to recognize a "Season of Joy," as our time to rejoice in the protections and blessings that God has bestowed upon His faithful. This is our *Sukkot*, the harvest-time festival of Tabernacles, which like what we call the season of Advent.

From this perspective, we are all Israelites, those who believe their promised Messiah has come. This means we should be able to see how Easter Sunday represents the first week of the Counting of the Omer, with the seven-week Easter Season being the seven weeks towards receipt of the rules and by-laws that bind our Agreement with God.

The *Shavuot* week (a two-day festival) is called the Festival of the First Fruits, such that the Israelites were the first fruits of the vine that would bear Jesus, as Christ. This means the Day of Pentecost is the time when the Good Fruits of Christ are ready and ripe to be the spiritual food for others to consume, as true servants of the Lord, filled with God's Holy Spirit.

We Receive the Spirit – as we heard read today when the risen body of Jesus told that to his disciples – when we accept God's laws to be written into our hearts.

That does not require memorization and mechanical compliance – as though we **ACT** because God told us by written Law.  To have God's Law written into one's heart requires one offer complete devotion, through the sacrifice of ourselves.  God, through the Christ Mind, makes all His Law be known instantly, without having to think about anything.  Knowing the Law "by heart" means a New Life has been brought into us divinely.

That was what the risen Lord said to his disciple … and it is what his Spirit says to us … Receive the Holy Spirit of Jesus, so that the mind of Jesus leads your thoughts, while the love of God fills your hearts.

Now, you must realize the disciples did not instantly all jump up when they heard Jesus say, "Peace be with you," shouting in unison, "And also with you!"

Imagine what would have taken place if Jesus had eleven Episcopalian disciples hidden away in the room, along with their wives and children.  Imagine if they all said "And also with you" in response to a command by Jesus.

Can you hear the audacity of that programmed response?

"**And**" is a statement that says "You **and** me, both."  It says, "I have the Holy Spirit," so I wish that state of being back upon you.

"Peace be with you Brother Jesus," is the meaning of that

Easter Sermons: Second Sunday of Easter, Year B

return.

John would have had to add some verses where Jesus looked aghast at the disciples and began scolding them, saying, "Listen to what I say and stop pretending you are strong followers … you who hide behind locked doors!"

The disciples included Thomas, who was not present when Jesus appeared that first Easter Sunday evening. Thomas represents all Christian disciples who require proof … of God, of Christ, of the Holy Spirit … before they can fully commit to becoming an Apostle … the Good Fruit that will become ripe and drop from the vine on the Day of Pentecost.

Jesus said, "Blessed are those who have not seen and yet have come to believe."

Still, that "Blessing of the LORD" comes from devotion that goes beyond simply walking behind a man that can be seen in the flesh. Such devotion requires preparation.

The forty days that Jesus appeared in the flesh, as the risen Lord, prepared the disciples to evolve into Apostles.

Those forty days took place during the tenth day of the Counting of the Omer, until the forty-ninth day. That equates to the Tuesday following Easter Sunday, until Jesus' Ascension on a Sabbath … after he and his disciples had travelled as far as allowed on that holy day of the week.

Think, for a moment, about the bookends surrounding Passover (or Holy Week) - forty days of Lent, followed by forty days of intensive training. Forty is a mystical number that represents a divine foundation (as ten times four). As Christians, the Lenten and Easter seasons are symbolic of the sacrifice God calls for us to make, in order to be reborn as His Sons (regardless of one's human gender).

After forty days preparing to go forty days learning from the Master, God then wrote his laws upon the hearts of devoted disciples at 9:00 AM, the Fiftieth day – the Day of Pentecost – so their full-pledged commitment to be priests for the One God began on a Holy Sunday.

This means today, the second Sunday of Easter … the Christian version of the Counting of the Omer … represents when **WE** are told by Christ Jesus to, "Receive the Holy Spirit."

Christ says to us to let "Peace be with us."

John wrote in his first epistle, "If we say we have no sin, we deceive ourselves, and the truth is not in us."

This means responding, "And so with you!" as if we have so much "peace" in our hearts we can give it away freely. We should, but ….

This response gives the <u>pretence</u> of being filled with the Holy Spirit, when that "Blessing" by God only fills those who become the unblemished Lamb of God.

The Easter Season has the meaning of learning how Jesus was prophesied in ALL of the Old Testament books, which can only be taught by one with the understanding of the Holy Spirit … as Jesus was, is, and will always be.

# Easter Sermons: Second Sunday of Easter, Year B

The Jews daily say a prayer and openly state what day it is, in the numbering of the days until the Law came down with Moses.

Christians should recognize this same commitment is expected of them, where each day of the Easter Season we pray for guidance to the Lord, as we study the words of the Holy Bible, so we may Receive the Spirit of understanding.

Only with devotion can we arise on the Day of Pentecost and like the sound of a rush of violent wind be filled with the Holy Spirit and begin ministering to those followers in need of assistance.

Only when we have been filled with the Holy Spirit can we begin **ACTS** as Apostles

When we recite:

Christ **has** died.

Christ **is** risen.

Christ **will come** again.

We recite the three phases of all time: Past, present, and future.

As it was, so it is, and so it will be again.

The meaning is this:

The flesh of Jesus **has** died.

Robert Tippett

The immortal soul of Jesus **is** spiritually risen.

The Spirit of Jesus **will** again **fill** the flesh that we sacrifice unto the LORD, so that each of our bodies can become reborn as Jesus again.

There is no waiting for the end of the world to come, in the sense that we imagine a return of Christ, who will appear as Jesus in the clouds. The end of our worlds, each individual world as a living body of flesh, comes when we open our souls up to receive the Holy Spirit that is Jesus Christ ...reborn into us, miraculously making each of us become Jesus reborn.

Christ **will come again** as **us**!

Christ **came again** as the Apostles!

Christ **has continuously come again** over the centuries, as long as Christians have devoted their selves to the will of God.

In the Counting of the Easter Omer, we are now on Day 8, just as Jesus was raised on a Sabbath that was the seventh day in the Counting of the Omer. Easter Sunday ... then and now ... is the eighth day in the counting. There are seven weeks in the Easter Season. Seven times seven is forty-nine.

We have reached the Second Sunday of Easter, so today is the fifteenth day in the counting of the forty-nine. Jesus ascended on the forty-ninth day ... a Sabbath. The disciples became Apostles - filled with the Holy Spirit of Christ - on the Fiftieth day ... a Sunday.

# Easter Sermons: Second Sunday of Easter, Year B

Just as Moses descended from the mountain on the fiftieth day - to offer the Israelites stone tablets with laws etched in them by the finger of God - Jesus will descend on the Day of Pentecost - to offer us the laws written on our hearts.

But ... as it was in both cases ... we have to make an Agreement ... a Covenant ... a Testament to the LORD and to Christ. We must Receive the Spirit, not just think it is a gift we place in a drawer and never experience.

Our redemption from slavery to sin will not be complete until we have received God in our hearts and Christ in each one of our minds.

Let us pray:

Today is two weeks and one day, as fifteen days towards the Omer – our measure as fruits of the Lord Jesus Christ – which culminates with our receipt of your Holy Spirit on the Day of Pentecost.

Guide us this day to learn from your words and find insight from you ... as the Word of Life ... so we may be strengthened in our devotion to God our LORD and His Holy Son, through the Holy Spirit.

Amen

# THIRD SUNDAY OF EASTER

# YEAR B

**Relevant readings:**
Acts 3:12-19
Psalm 4   1
John 3:1-7
Luke 24:36b-48

## Walking in the name of the Lord

Last week we ended with a prayer representing a counting of the Easter Omer. Today is the Third Sunday of the Easter Season, meaning twenty-two days have passed since Our Lord was offered to the Temple as a sacrifice to God.

Let us pray:

# Easter Sermons: Third Sunday of Easter, Year B

Today is three weeks and one day, as twenty-two days towards the Omer – our measure as fruits of the Lord Jesus Christ – which culminates with our receipt of your Holy Spirit on the Day of Pentecost.

Guide us this day to learn from your words and find insight from you ... as the Word of Life ... so we may be strengthened in our devotion to God our LORD and His Holy Son, through the Holy Spirit.

Amen

It is important for Christians to adopt a new tradition, which accepts the Israelites' Counting of the Omer. It is not done without reason ... with the simplest reason being: A daily counting by the faithful is a sign of obedience to a rule of ritual.

For Jews today, it represents a dedication to "re-living" the moments in time, from the freedom from bondage in Egypt until the receipt of the Law of Moses.

Counting the Omer is their obedience to an external rule of ritual that expresses faith in the One God.

As Episcopalians, we partake of the body and blood of Christ because of a new external rule of ritual, commanded by Jesus when he said, "Do this in remembrance of me."

Jesus **added** to the existing external ritual by saying, "When you do this (as commanded by God)," then remember his role acting as part of that ritual observance.

Counting the Easter Omer then becomes a Christian obedience to an external rule of ritual that expresses faith in the One God **AND** belief that the promised Messiah has come.

This means that a Christian Counting of the Easter Omer is also in remembrance of the timing of when Jesus Ascended – on the forty-ninth day – with the Holy Spirit coming upon the Apostles on the Day of Pentecost (the Fiftieth day). The Day of Pentecost is when the Law of God becomes written on one's heart ... when one truly becomes Christian.

By doing a ritual that is suggested, or recommended, <u>through external rule</u>, the **purpose** is to ingrain the external rule <u>internally</u>.

We hear it said of the Eucharist that it is, "An outward and visible sign of an inward and spiritual grace."

We need to be sure we realize that saying does not mean: When one kneels at an altar to eat a wafer and sip some sweet wine, one becomes filled with inner peace.

The reason the Israelites count the days until God presented them with His Law is it took **time** for that to happen. They had to **act** as instructed to survive the Passover. They had to follow Moses when he led them out of Egypt. They had to cross through the dry land that had been (and would soon be again) covered with sea water. They had to **ACT** first; before they could receive **THE FIRST REWARD** for being God's chosen people – a Binding Covenant of Agreement.

As a child, I played Hide and Seek. There are rules to that game. In order to let the hiders have time to hide without being seen, the seeker has to cover his or her eyes and count to 50 out loud.

To children, it seems that speeding up the count will make it easier to catch someone who is still not fully hidden, when the count is finished.

Children like to bend the external rules, even while still following them.

Speedily they count out loud: "One, two, three, four, five, six, seven, eighteen, twenty, forty-five, FIFTY! Ready or not, here I come!"

The childish mind is so excited about playing the game that it hurries to do all the external rules, because the **ACT** of seeking is the fun part. The rules limit how soon that fun can begin.

Adults also have the same childish mind, especially when it comes to following the rules.

Who hasn't seen a speed limit sign posting a specific speed as simply a "recommendation" of what some think a safe speed is?

The sign says "55," but: It **is** light out; It is **not** raining; and There's not much traffic around.

Hmmmm?

Who does **not** force oneself to drive **under** that maximum speed limit?

It is the childlike mind within us that thinks nothing of bending the external rules.

It is important to hear John talking about the "**children** of God" and see how he was talking to us, here today.

WE are those who "play the game" of Christianity, with the external rules only limiting that pleasure.

WE want so much to be filled with the Holy Spirit that we speed past all the external rules and pretend we have **IT** …

… until we realize **IT** does not feel special.

**IT** is not what corner-cutters would call "an inward and spiritual grace."

**IT** is not what childlike minds imagine IT would be like.

**IT** feels like **IT** is not there.

**IT** feels like the disciples felt after Jesus had been killed on a cross … cold and empty … frightening … not a fun game anymore.

**IT** is there, however. You have to do more than follow the rules to get to where you can truly find **IT**.

Last week we read from John's first epistle, where he wrote, "My <u>little children</u>, I am writing these things to you so that you may not sin."

John was **not** actually writing to young children, under the age of twelve.

Today, from the same letter we read John say, "Little children, let no one deceive you."

John also wrote, "No one who abides in him sins."

He continued to say, "Everyone who does what is right is righteous, just as he is righteous."

Letters are like rules being explained. The letters of the Apostles – especially those of Paul, but also those by Peter and John – are difficult to understand and often need to be explained.

In this last explanation written by John, the key word, which might be overlooked, is "does." "Everyone who **does** what is right is righteous."

Another way of saying that is, "Everyone who **ACTS** right is righteous."

**ACTING** right says you followed all the rules **AND** you found **IT**.

Too often we see ourselves as righteous, when we have "**done**" nothing "right." We only <u>know</u> the rules. We <u>know</u> how the game is played. But, we never <u>know</u> the true satisfaction that is supposed to come from "playing the game."

This is because Jesus Christ is left out of our equation. We do not "**abide** in Jesus."

Think about that for a moment. "We do not **abide** in Jesus."

The Greek word written that is translated as "abides" is "*menōn*" (which comes from the verb "*menó*"), meaning (in the third person singular) "remains, abides, stays, waits."

This means that we "live" within the framework that is Jesus. The rules are to **do** EVERYTHING as Jesus **did** and would **do** today.

We know that our bodies are the temple of the soul, but to "**abide** in Jesus" means to assume the life of the Son of God. His life becomes a reproduction in our life.

We are expected ... as Christians ... to "remain in Jesus" character, making **HIM** become the model for our complete way of life.

**CELL CYCLE / CELL DIVISION**

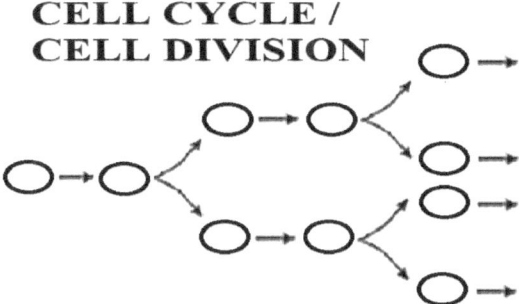

Jesus enters us and we pass Jesus onto others, just as all cells in one body share the same DNA. Many cells, one body, one code to life.

That can only happen if we stop ACTING for ourselves, and start ACTING as Jesus would **ACT**, if Jesus were taking up residence within us.

Now, in the story we heard today from the Book of the Acts of the Apostles, we learn how astonished Peter was because

# Easter Sermons: Third Sunday of Easter, Year B

the Jews in the Temple had seen "the lame man healed."

Jesus likewise healed many people, including the lame. However, if you listen to what Peter said, you see how little Peter did, and we can remember just how little Jesus did when people were healed.

Peter said, "By faith in his name, his name alone has made this man strong." He had been crippled from birth, and was carried to the gate of the temple to beg for alms.

The lame beggar had asked Peter for money, but Peter said all he had was the name of Jesus Christ. The man reached out to take Peter's hand, just as he would reach out and take money from strangers. When Peter touched the lame beggar he stood, walked, and even leaped with joy.

The lame man **ACTED** from faith in Jesus being the Christ of the One God. Peter **ACTED** from faith to move someone in need, as the hand that offered Jesus, who abided within him.

In the Gospel of Luke, we read of Jesus standing among his disciples and their companions. This happened right after Cleopas and his wife, Mary, returned to Jerusalem to find the eleven disciples (in hiding). They had returned to tell them they had seen the Lord in their home, in Emmaus.

Jesus then appeared, like a ghost ... without opening any doors. Jesus asked those male followers who trembled, "Why are you frightened, and why do doubts arise in your hearts?"

Think about that in comparison to the lame beggar who was

healed at the gate to the temple.

I imagine, if anyone had an excuse to fear getting up and walking, it would be someone crippled from birth, who had to be carried and set where he could beg for alms. If anyone would doubt someone telling him to stop begging and get up, it would be him.

But the beggar immediately got up and walked ... simply because Peter said all he had was "**faith**," which had become strengthened by his becoming Peter "**in his name**." The name of Jesus Christ had been reborn in Peter, giving Peter true faith.

When the lame beggar touched Peter **in the name** of Jesus Christ, the **faith** of the lame beggar meant he too was Jesus reborn. He got up and walked.

The disciples did not have true faith, even though they had said over and over that they believed in Jesus.

People say they believe in the Law too ... that external and visible document that says, "Do this, and don't do that."

But, how many people have heard, "Ignorance of the law is no excuse for breaking the law?" We love to play ignorant ... meaning we love to ignore, because awareness brings with it responsibility.

To the disciples, Jesus was just an external law. He told the disciples what to do, and they did it ... sometimes (like children) grumbling under their breath and not liking being told to do some things.

# Easter Sermons: Third Sunday of Easter, Year B

So, with Jesus dead, they were afraid they would get sentenced to death too. Then, there was the ghost of Jesus, come to condemn them for being afraid. So, they shook even more.

We have to be able to see the same childish fear is why we are not **ACTING** as Jesus would have us. It is our fear that prevents us from filled with the Holy Spirit.

WE are **not** telling crippled people to walk in the name of Jesus Christ ... at least with any real conviction that there is any power behind those words.

We can't even make ourselves walk without sin.

Now, Jesus "opened [the disciples'] minds to understand scriptures." That is the first **ACT** everyone who claims to be a Christian **MUST** do, before he or she can be filled with the presence of Jesus' mind. That is actually one of the seven gifts of the Holy Spirit ... understanding prophecy; but it is impossible to understand what one never bothers to learn. The season of Easter is ALL about taking that step.

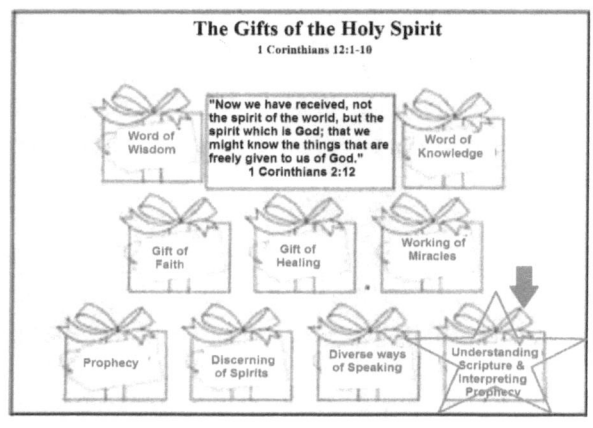

You **MUST** be able to understand the depth of meaning that is written into the words you have heard before ... but never gave much thought about.

That is how children "play the game" of faith. "It is something too great for my little brain."

I remember as a child I drew a lot of pictures while in the pew of my church, while the preacher gave a sermon. He did not talk in childish terms that I could follow. I went to Sunday school and learned the children's version of the Bible stories, which was fun.

But, the preacher did not speak on my childish mind's level ... so I tuned him out and drew pictures.

The disciples knew a similar childish version of the writings that led them to faith ... the stories and songs they had memorized ... but that was not enough to keep them from a fear of everything <u>except God</u>.

But ... how many adults are little more than children in larger bodies, sitting in pews tuning out, never hearing Jesus calling them to grow up and be Jesus-like?

You have to take your faith seriously, from an adult perspective, if you plan on God taking your soul seriously when it comes time to judge your life. God **knows** how much and how little your **ACTS** have been for Him ... and for whatever reasons.

You have to see how there is no one who is going to carry you to church each Sunday, so you can beg for alms from Christ, using every excuse in the book about how crippled you are, and explaining how you deserve credit for having gone that far.

You would probably complain that walking on your own is too much work ... too hard an ACT to accomplish ... rather than have enough faith to get up and leap with joy.

You see, there is no law that says you must learn everything written in the Holy Bible. There is no law that says you must come to church prepared to pass a test each Sunday.

In that regard, a state of lawlessness exists.

John wrote in his epistle, "Everyone who commits sin is guilty of lawlessness; sin is lawlessness."

Because you do not have the laws of God written on your hearts ... because you don't have the mind of Christ setting the rules for the house you abide in (the body of your soul) ... you go the route of least resistance ... lawlessness. In that sense, lawlessness is sloth – a deadly sin.

It is easier to sleep-in on Sunday, than it is to wake up earlier and go to Sunday school for adults. It is certainly easier to go and say nothing, add nothing of value to an adult discussion.

And to teach an adult Sunday school class? Forget about it!

It is easier to listen to people explain the meanings of the Scriptures .. and doubt you have anything to offer ... than it is to talk to others about what scriptures mean to you ... when you never thought about Scriptures as something the lay folk need to know.

It is easier to be Christian whenever you feel like it, than it is to **ACT** Christian ... 24-7 ... full time responsible.

There is nothing that says a Christian must do anything that God told the Israelites to do ... because you have lived a crippled religious life since birth ... thinking you are "saved," without any need to change.

Peter told the lame beggar, "In the name of Jesus Christ of Nazareth, walk."

He believed. He walked because of faith. He walked because he became **in the name of Jesus Christ**!

Jesus spent 40 days showing the disciples how to read the scriptures properly. He explained how to understand the meaning behind words that prophesied his birth, death, resurrection, ascension, and return.

Seeing that amazing story unfold before your eyes ... seeing it for **yourself**, on your own, with no one telling you what to think ... is as much proof of God ... of Jesus as Christ ... as it would be if Jesus were to appear right now before us, showing us his flesh and bones, asking for some broiled fish to eat.

Just as you coax a baby to learn to walk, gently assisting it so it won't fall too hard, giving it less and less help ... out of love ... babies learn to walk by testing their own capabilities. They fear walking, but have to learn not to fear what they were born to do.

Once learned, we all forget ever having been taught how to

walk on our own.

Babies do not learn to walk and then regress to crawling the rest of its life, wasting a God-given talent.

The Easter Season is when we learn to walk, so we can receive the Holy Spirit on the Day of Pentecost. When we have received **IT**, then we can truly know the meaning of how Jesus is "an outward and visible sign of an inward and spiritual grace."

Little children, in the name of Jesus Christ of Nazareth, walk.

Amen

# FOURTH SUNDAY OF EASTER

# YEAR B

**Relevant readings:**
Acts 4:5-12
Psalm 23
1 John 3:16-24
John 10:11-18

## A school for good shepherds

The last two weeks we have incorporated a prayer into the service that represents a counting of the Easter Omer. Today is the Fourth Sunday of the Easter Season, meaning twenty-nine days have passed since Our Lord was offered to the Temple as a sacrifice to God.

Easter Sermons: Fourth Sunday of Easter, Year B

Let us pray:

Today is four weeks and one day, as twenty-nine days towards the Omer – our measure as fruits of the Lord Jesus Christ – which culminates with our receipt of your Holy Spirit on the Day of Pentecost.

Guide us this day to learn from your words and find insight from you ... as the Word of Life ... so we may be strengthened in our devotion to God our LORD and His Holy Son, through the Holy Spirit.

Amen

Today has a name, as far as the lectionary is concerned. You may have picked up on it from the bulletin or noticed the repeated theme coming from the readings. Today is called "Good Shepherd Sunday."

Today we read Psalm 23 – "The LORD is my shepherd ...."

We also read from John, where Jesus said, "I am the good shepherd."

It should be understood that "Good Shepherd Sunday" does not coincidentally fall now, during the season of Easter ... amid the counting of the Easter Omer.

It should also be understood that the lectionary for each Sunday normally includes: an Old Testament reading, a psalm, an Epistle reading, and a Gospel reading.

It is not coincidence, that beginning Easter Sunday and

continuing throughout the Easter Season, including the Sunday of Pentecost, we have replaced the Old Testament reading with readings from the Book of the Acts of the Apostles.

All of this is planned, with purpose.

The Easter Season is focused on the **ACTS** of those who had been disciples of the most-holy man named Jesus of Nazareth. It would be those followers who would be transformed into Apostles, as demonstrated by their righteous acts.

The eleven added a twelfth from those who were likewise disciples of Jesus, just not on his 'executive board' and all would become themselves most-holy men (and women). They would gain this benefit by witnessing the resurrection of the Christ and learning from him for forty days afterwards. That diligence of faith was rewarded when they were given the Holy Spirit on the Fiftieth Day.

The Holy Spirit is why the disciples **ACTED** as Apostles. Without **ACTS**, a disciple is nothing more than a student unprepared to stand and walk alone.

In fact, the four Gospels could be called "The <u>ACTS of Jesus Christ</u>," as recalled by Matthew, Mark, Luke, and John. Jesus **did** many things before his death, including healing and preaching, with all his **ACTS** for the benefit of others.

Thus, we must see that "Good Shepherd Sunday" is not about reminiscing … not about how we should always recall how Jesus is, was, and will forever be **the** "Good Shepherd" … and not about sitting mutely as a disciple, thinking you are being asked to believe Jesus was a gift from God that can never be duplicated.

Instead, "Good Shepherd Sunday" coming during the Counting of the Easter Omer period is designed to point out how the Apostles – this week Peter and John (brother of James, of father Zebedee) – were themselves "Good Shepherds," as seen in the text from the Book of Acts. They were graduates of the "Jesus Basic Training Program for Disciples who will become Apostles."

Therefore, you sit here listening and you are immersed by words that set a course for **you**.

**YOU** are called by Jesus to be a Good Shepherd ... just as he was and is ... just as the Apostles were and still are ... as new Apostles ... new Good Shepherds.

In the story we read in Acts today, which is a continuation of last week's healing of a lame beggar outside the Temple, Peter and John are now found arrested and brought before the Sanhedrin.

Peter told them – as did Jesus, not too long before Peter addressed that assembly – "The stone that was rejected by you, the builders; it has become the cornerstone."

Peter, then added, "There is salvation in no one else." That, of course, means Jesus was-is-will always be the cornerstone of every human 'tabernacle' to God. Therefore, Jesus saves and **that** is the only way to heaven.

This is read today because in John's Gospel (John not born of Zebedee) we read of Jesus saying, "The hired hand, who is not the shepherd and does not own the sheep, sees the wolf coming and leaves the sheep and runs away."

This is the same as a "builder" as a "hired hand," rather than a priest who serves a flock as an extension of God. A 'hired builder' would see a perfect "cornerstone," from which a solid structure could be built - one that would last forever - as a reason to reject it ... or be afraid to face no longer being needed as a 'hired builder'. Fear would cause such a builder to reject that perfect cornerstone's use, because using an imperfect cornerstone would forever require further need for a "builder" to fix something. Should the building totally collapse, killing everyone inside, then that 'hired hand builder' would leave those 'sheep' and run away.

In a sense, the builder who chooses the perfect cornerstone is like a Good Shepherd that builds a perfect sheepfold, one that keeps the wolves out. Such a sheepfold "structure" can now be seen as the school Jesus built that trained disciples to become Apostles.

Anyone <u>less</u> than a "good builder" would become as worthless as a "hired shepherd," always coming back to oversee quick fixes to the poor structure originally designed, or running away from lawsuits charging malpractice.

It says the temple hierarchy of the Church of Judaism was not connected to God – it knew it – and it didn't care that it wasn't – as it was only in that position of quasi-power because it was profitable ... on a material plane. The Sanhedrin was nothing more than "hired hands," where "hired" says they were paid to serve.

Easter Sermons: Fourth Sunday of Easter, Year B

If you listen very carefully, or if you read <u>and re-read</u> this passage about the Good Shepherd and the hired hands, you can see deeper meaning coming from Jesus saying, "There will be one flock, one shepherd."

You can quickly read that and think, "The one shepherd is Jesus, with the one flock being all Christians." That would be true, in one sense; but that is not the intent or the whole truth.

In Psalm 23 ... the one psalm of David that most Christians memorize and easily recognize ... we recall, "The **LORD** is my shepherd."

The "one shepherd" is then YHWH, the One God. Realizing that means one can see Jesus as "one flock," or a flock of one, who had the "one shepherd" within him, through the Holy Spirit of God.

Thus, Jesus the Good Shepherd always said, "Truthfully, I speak what God has me say," as the 'mouth of God' on the physical plane.

The Counting of the first Easter Omer was forty-nine days, with the last forty being after Jesus was risen (on day seven in that count - a Sabbath). Jesus showed himself as risen to his disciples on day eight of that count - a Sunday. Jesus then spent his remaining time with his disciples, preparing them to realize the full intent of his words, "There will be one flock, one shepherd."

Each individual disciple had then (and has now) to come to the realization that "**I AM the one flock**," when YHWH is within me ... **AS ME**.

Sheep need a shepherd to be nearby ... on the hillside overlooking the meadow below, where the sheep happily graze without a care in the world.  Thus, physical sheep depend on an **EXTERNAL** protector.

Sheep are then like disciples ... totally dependent on a leader.

A "hired hand" is then an "external protector;" but a "hired hand" is one who does not "own the sheep."  Therefore, a "hired hand" is one who will not "lay down his life for the sheep."

The word "sheep" denotes both the singular and plural number.  That means a <u>flock of sheep</u> is **one** or it is **many**.

When you see yourself as "a sheep," as one in a "flock of sheep," then you only think in terms, "Mmmmmm, I am so looking forward to grazing today.  I am going to enjoy the sweet taste of fine earthly grasses and shrubs, and the cool refreshing delight of waters from the mountain's streams and cisterns.  I look forward to leaping and playing and doing nothing other than meeting my own needs."

As "a sheep," you never think about the safety of others. You only depend on someone other than you to protect you from harm's way.

As a Christian, we are just like this.  Those who come to church (still), do so to listen and be seen with the flock, leaving all the shepherding to the priest, minister, or preacher.  After all, "He or she studied to do sermons, so it is not up to me to question anything, much less challenge anything."

However, in that position you are then ALWAYS at the mercy of "hired hands," because ... after all ... regardless of who it is that leads you to green pastures and still waters, it is **YOU** that has to take in all **YOU** can.

Regardless of which "hired hands" told you the things you wanted to hear, and which "hired hands" turned out to be snakes, or which "hired hands" you hated to see leave ... **ANYONE** who is not <u>you</u> is nothing more than external protection ... a "hired hand."

No one in this world, other than you, is ever going to eat your food or drink your water for you. On the contrary, a hired hand is more apt to strip you of your value (fleece your wool) and every once in a while slit your throat and eat your mutton, using your skin to make coats.

In that sense, external shepherds ... bad shepherds ... false shepherds ... they can only possess you ... own you ... <u>on the material plane</u>.

That is why God and Christ seek to own the true you ... your soul ... so God and Christ can make **YOU** "one flock," with "one shepherd" within you, through the presence of the Holy Spirit.

To give up ownership of yourself, you have to lay down your life for the flock that is **YOU**. **YOU** have to let go of being a sheep and let God and Christ transform you into a Good Shepherd.

You have to stop being a disciple and start being an Apostle.

Not too long ago, I read an article posted on a blog, which was addressing why "Millennials" were leaving the Church. The article was written by a "Millennial," from a perspective that expressed one person's opinion as to why that Millennial no longer saw the Church as appealing. Thoughts on the matter then led that person to draw conclusions as to what changes could be made to the Episcopal Church, in order to bring back the young folk.

Basically ... and I am paraphrasing now, but not too wildly ... the author's solution was: "Make Church less like school and more like a coffee house."

That person made a comment (similar to), "Many millennials are in college and spend so much time learning away from Church, the last thing they want to do is go to some place where they have to learn some more." The recommendation went on to suggest "high quality coffee, not the cheap stuff."

In short, this youngster suggested the Church should stop being a Church and become a social group.

<pause>

Unfortunately ... that change happened LONG ago and that is why millennials ... and so many others ... are leaving the Church today.

I have seen the churches of other denominations cater to more of that environment of **entertainment**, which can be called "The Millennial Church." If you have never been to one, then let me describe what it is:

First you have upholstered "stadium seating," not wood pews. There are cup holders in the armrests - for coffee that is sold at the refreshment center outside the amphitheatre. The hymnals are absent, replaced with a big screen television above the 'stage' that displays the song lyrics, along with a bouncing ball, whenever it is time to sing. Rather than old dusty standards sung, the band performs something like 'alternative rock' Gospel songs, performed with a dancing choir. The leader of these Millennial Churches are always cool, thirty-something (maybe early forties) preacher, who energetically does a performance "in the round," with a "hands free" microphone headset. There is no lectionary to follow along with, as the theme seems to always be about getting rich with Christ.

Some of these preachers do take their sermon notes with them as they walk about ... using the latest smart phone in one hand to be their reference. A physical Bible to read from is optional for the other hand. The people are often called upon to turn to a page in their Bibles (not supplied by the church), but it rarely is to teach about the meaning of Scripture.

All that makes going to church fun for the younger folk ... but even with all the extra bells and whistles ... if you only go for the music and dancing, then you are missing the point of why people go to a church.

The problem is **not** that a Church teaches too much. The problem is that no one sees a church as a school ... as a place of learning.

Robert Tippett

After all, what is the purpose of going to school?

It is to learn ... to pass tests ... to graduate ... to eventually move on to a career, where one's education can then be applied in the real "grown-up" world of **life**.

We see education as a means for possessing things. It is therefore seen as a **NEED**. Millennials see education in a school setting as the perfect cornerstone to their life happiness (until the student loans come in). They see the Church as unnecessary. To desire a church with a theatre atmosphere is to desire one built with an imperfect cornerstone; one built to collapse.

To see a man of thirty-something going to school full-time, having been in school since he was eighteen ... still not in possession of even an Associate's degree ... much less a Bachelor's degree ... far from the seriousness of seeking a Graduate degree program to enter ... that man would be seen in a negative light.

People would whisper (minimally), "Get a job! Stop trying to be a child all your life! Grow up!"

Well, Church is meant to be a place of higher learning.

Millennials see the pointlessness of never moving beyond "pew burn," with gold and silver stars for attendance in no way being better than sleeping-in on Sunday. They have dropped out of Church School because their education says going to church is illogical.

Those who are growing old with the Church (the parents and grandparents of Millennials) are seen by the millennials as being just like that imaginary thirty-something man who forever pretends to go to school ... for whatever selfish purposes ... but never graduates.

The same people attend church "classes" on some basis, be it regular, semi-regular, sporadic, or rare occasions, but they never graduate! They see a church 'education' pointless, because attendance is the only need. Going to church becomes one's right to claim status as an enrollee. As long as one does not get "expelled" (some call it "excommunication") then going to church means forever being a card-carrying Christian (where the card says, "Admit one into Heaven").

Still, few hear a sermon is if it were a lecture given by a professor in a college course, where paying attention could be the difference between passing or failing an exam. In an Episcopal church, one sermon is one small piece of a three-year cycle of classes, which should be seen in the same light. With proper study and application realized as the intended purpose of spiritual learning, then going to church should be as life rewarding as going to college.

With a Good Shepherd preaching good sermons, then a good student of religion will be led to self-sufficiency (minimally). That then can lead to 'graduate studies', where one regularly attends Bible Studies or lectionary classes ... even teaching others in classes like those (like a Graduate Assistant). Going to church to learn should be the fun part of going to church.

Unfortunately, most see there are no tests to pass from going to church, no reasons to write down notes, no reasons to be able to become Bible self-sufficient. This sad state is because no one sees a reason to graduate.

No big deal. No one is ever going to judge me for that lack of applied faith.

<pause>

Now, excuse me while I step up onto the "Fire and Brimstone" soapbox.

I rise higher before you, looking down upon you, just so I can state loudly, "Look at what is in the news every day!"

I don't even need to list anything specific from the news. Just think of what you have heard in the last weeks ... months ... years.

<pause>

Does the world seem to be headed towards another sunny day of grazing in green pastures, and sipping from still waters?

Or, does the world seem to be headed towards darkness, where our children no longer want to go to church to learn, because their parents never learned why they went to church from their parents?

<step down off soapbox>

Okay, enough of the end of the world talk and back to the purpose of today's fourth Sunday of Easter **LESSON**.

You have to see how Jesus is talking to **YOU** ... every time

Easter Sermons: Fourth Sunday of Easter, Year B

Jesus says anything.

When Jesus said, "I have other sheep that do not belong to this fold," he was talking about your neighbors, your family, your friends, your employers, your enemies. **YOU** are one flock with God and Jesus as **YOUR** good shepherd, but God and Jesus want everyone else to be a singular sheep flock, just like **YOU**.

Therefore, when Jesus said, "I must bring them also, and they will listen to my voice," you have to realize that the voice of Christ is **YOU** … when Christ is within **YOU**, through **YOUR** receipt of God's Holy Spirit. Jesus speaks to those other flocks through **YOU**!

The lessons are important because, just like the disciples had Christ spend forty days opening their eyes to the deeper meaning of the Scriptures, those lessons do make sense. Those were lessons they had learned since childhood and knew … but never understood the depth of meaning that was there.

For lessons to reach that point of epiphany some prior effort has to have been made … at least to have heard them before … even if half asleep … as the Gospels portray how slow-witted the disciples often were.

You have to have gone to school; you have to remain active in school, before there is hope to graduate from school.

You have to prove to your professors … God and Christ … that you can handle the deeper meaning, from having learned the simpler story.

You cannot go home and pray, "God, PLEASE make me wake up tomorrow as a doctor" ... or lawyer ... or architect ... or computer programmer ... or anything that requires an education ... and then blame God if you wake up to the same **YOU**.

God will answer your prayers with the opportunity to gain the education you need ... for God to lead you where you can best serve God.

Everyone here is a flock of one. Everyone here is called to be a Good Shepherd, which means being led by God in your heart and Christ in your mind, because only God and Christ are the "one shepherd of the one flock."

On the Day of Pentecost ... now only three weeks away ... each of **YOU** is called to lay down your life and let the Holy Spirit enter.

If you can make that commitment ... if you can make that sacrifice ... then you can say, as did Jesus, "For this reason the Father loves me, because I lay down my life in order to take it up again."

Jesus will be reborn as **YOU**, and at that time you will fully understand how John said, "All who obey his commandments abide in him, and he abides in them."

To live there, you have to be a house built with the perfect cornerstone.

Amen

# Easter Sermons: Fourth Sunday of Easter, Year B

# FIFTH SUNDAY OF EASTER

# YEAR B

**Relevant readings:**
Acts 8:26-40
Psalm 22:24-31
1 John 4:7-21
John 15:1-8

## Released into the wilderness as a purposeful branch of the true living vine

Over the last three weeks, beginning the second Sunday of Easter, we have incorporated a prayer into the service that represents a counting of the Easter Omer. Today is the Fifth Sunday of the Easter Season, meaning thirty-six days have passed since Our Lord was offered to the Temple as a sacrifice to God.

Let us pray:

Today is five weeks and one day, as thirty-six days towards the Omer – our measure as fruits of the Lord Jesus Christ – which culminates with our receipt of your Holy Spirit on the Day of Pentecost.

Guide us this day to learn from your words and find insight from you ... as the Word of Life ... so we may be strengthened in our devotion to God our LORD and His Holy Son, through the Holy Spirit.

Amen

In the Acts reading for today, we find an Ethiopian eunuch reading from Isaiah's fifty-third chapter, verses seven and eight. As he reads, he is being sped along a wilderness road headed to Gaza.

Another way of presenting the translation of this reading states it this way:

> **He** was oppressed and afflicted,
>
> yet **he** did not open **his** mouth;
>
> **he** was led like a lamb to the slaughter,
>
> and as a sheep before its shearers is silent,
>
> so **he** did not open **his** mouth.

From arrest and judgment **he** was taken away.

Yet who of **his** generation protested?

For **he** was cut off from the land of the living;

for the transgression of my people **he** was punished.

To better grasp why the Ethiopian eunuch would ask Philip, "About whom does the prophet say this?" it helps to know that Isaiah's chapter never says who "**he**" is.

Isaiah 53 begins by asking:

**Who** has **believed** our message and **to whom** has **the arm of the Lord** been revealed?

The rest of the verses then answer that question; but the verses written prior to seven and eight makes what the eunuch could not see be clearer to us today.

Using the same presentation format, Isaiah then wrote:

**He** grew up before **him** like a tender shoot, and like a root out of dry ground.

**He** had no beauty or majesty to attract us to **him**, nothing in **his** appearance that we should desire **him**.

**He** was despised and rejected by mankind, a man of suffering, and familiar with pain.

Like one from whom people hide their faces **he** was

> despised, and we held **him** in low esteem.
>
> Surely **he** took up our pain and bore our suffering, yet we considered **him** punished by God, stricken by **him**, and afflicted.
>
> But **he** was pierced for our transgressions, **he** was crushed for our iniquities; the punishment that brought us peace was on **him**, and by **his** wounds we are healed.
>
> We all, like sheep, have gone astray, each of us has turned to our own way;
>
> and the Lord has laid on **him** the iniquity of us all.

When you read these first eight verses of Isaiah 53 it is easy to see one person being identified, but only in the general sense. So, who is **he**?

Such a question gains importance when one reads, "We all have gone astray."

We have to feel the guilt of those who have sinned, but got off free, because someone else suffered for those sins.

But, who? Was it the author, Isaiah? Or, was it about some other prophet?

He was <u>pierced</u> for our transgressions.

He was <u>crushed</u> for our iniquities.

It is worthwhile to realize that sin was nothing new when

Jesus lived. Sin existed from the earliest moments the Israelites were led into the wilderness by Moses. Sin existed before Adam's original sin.

In Leviticus 16 we find God's response to the sins of Aaron and the sins of the Israelite people being addressed.

Verses 20 to 22 come after God has commanded that a bull and a goat be slaughtered and sacrificed by Aaron – the high priest. For Aaron's sins, the bull would be sacrificed. For the sins of the people, a goat would be sacrificed.

Afterwards, God gave these instructions:

> "When Aaron has finished making atonement for the Most Holy Place, the tent of meeting and the altar, he shall bring forward the live goat. He is to lay both hands on the head of the live goat and confess over it all the wickedness and rebellion of the Israelites—all their sins—and put them on the goat's head. He shall send the goat away into the wilderness in the care of someone appointed for the task. The goat will carry on itself all their sins to a remote place; and the man shall release it in the wilderness."

We call that the scapegoat, which is still part of the Day of Atonement in Israel.

In fact, verse 29 of Leviticus 16 tells how God said, "This is to be a lasting ordinance for you." So, the scapegoat is an every year symbolic release by the Jews, releasing a year's worth of sin on the head of a goat.

Isaiah foresaw a Jew replacing this scapegoat, who would

have the sins of all Israelites placed on his head. Jesus can then be seen in this light.

It would seem, to me that it is easier to be a scapegoat than it is to be a sacrificial lamb ... or a bull or a goat ... being slaughtered because of the sins of the people.

Jesus was slaughtered for that purpose, and few people would volunteer to suffer what Jesus suffered, before he gave up his life for the sins of the people.

However, if you are asked to take on the sins of the people ... without punishment and suffering ... more than just being released in some desolate place ... I think more people would opt for that ... if given a choice.

Still, if you listened carefully to that last instruction given by God to Aaron, the scapegoat, with all the sins of the people on its head, is set free in the wilderness.

This takes us back to the Ethiopian eunuch and Philip, who met over Isaiah 53 being read <u>in the wilderness</u>.

During this Eastertide, as with all Easter Omer counting periods, we learn how the disciples were transformed into Apostles. We sense how they were filled with the Holy Spirit and enabled to **ACT** in ways as Jesus had, prior to his being sacrificed.

In today's reading from the Book of the Acts of the Apostles we can see how Philip did similar things as Jesus. He caused an Ethiopian court official to rejoice, having been baptized with the Holy Spirit.

Philip then suddenly disappeared, as did Jesus ... more than once ... but in particular after he broke the bread with Cleopas and Mary in Emmaus. Just as they were amazed by being touched by the Holy Spirit, so too was the Ethiopian Eunuch.

What we should also see is how Philip was in a wilderness of ancient Judah, prior to beginning his ministry.

This is just like how Jesus spent his forty days in the wilderness prior to beginning his service to God, also after he had been filled with the Holy Spirit, when baptized by John.

You have to see this story represents a duplication of Jesus in Philip.

And that is important because of the reading from John's Gospel , about when Jesus told his disciples, "I am the true vine."

Jesus said, "I am the vine, you are the branches." Philip was a branch of that vine.

Prior to saying that, Jesus said, "Every branch that bears fruit [God the Father, the vine grower] prunes to make it bear more fruit." Philip bore the fruit of his ministry by baptizing the Ethiopian eunuch, making him become a new branch of the vine.

God planted the true vine, who was Jesus. Jesus, as the true vine, became a branch bearing fruit. Jesus spent three years healing people and preaching morals. He confronted those who led without vision, as false leaders.

Then, Jesus touched at least seventy who became his "great commission," but most of those fruit were taken before they could themselves "go to seed" and produce fruit.

The true vine of Jesus grew branches, which would become extensions of him. Jesus produced eleven disciples, who would become Apostles.

One of those branches was Philip.

Philip, in this story from Acts, was a branch that bore the fruit that was the Ethiopian eunuch.

That first fruit took place before Philip left the wilderness and began his ministry along the Mediterranean coast of ancient Israel and Judah.

When Philip became an evangelist, he had been pruned by God so he could bear more fruit.

Still, for a moment let's go back to the scapegoat story and look at the symbolism, so we can see that Jesus was the slaughtered goat. He died to atone for the sins of the people, meaning Philip represented the scapegoat that was sent out into the wilderness, also for the sins of the people.

God told Aaron to send the scapegoat out into the wilderness "in the care of someone appointed for the task." Do you recall how, "An angel of the Lord said to Philip, "Go"?

Philip was not alone up until that point when he was set free.

Philip, like the scapegoat, had the sins of the people on his head.

But think about that for a minute ... placing the sins of the people on the head of a goat.

<pause>

How do you think that would make the goat feel ... knowing it bore the responsibility of all the Israelites?

Do you think the goat felt sorry?

Or, do you think the goat felt glad he could be of service?

Or, do you think that goats really don't think like humans, and never feel any human emotions like guilt?

Consider this then: Isaiah wrote, "We all, <u>like sheep</u>, have gone astray, each of us has turned to our own way."

So, perhaps goats do think and feel responsibility ... when metaphor is understood.

Goats and sheep (considered to be in the same category of animal) go astray and go their own way, just as humans willfully sin.

The gesture of the Day of Atonement (which is the third commanded observance in a liturgical year – similar to our Advent) is forgiveness of sins. Thus, Philip was saving people, just as Jesus had.

Philip saved the Ethiopian eunuch by giving him the gift of

Easter Sermons: Fifth Sunday of Easter, Year B

the Holy Spirit, in the name of Christ.

Jesus saved Philip, by giving him the gift of the Holy Spirit, as the Son of God ... the true vine of the vine grower.

Each of the Apostles had a story like Philip's, whether we know those stories or not.

We would not be here today if they did not get set free in the wilderness areas of Judea and then set out making sure that atonement of others came to be apostles. Everyone needs to have a personal awareness of one's own sins ... have them be placed on one's head ... in order for one to bear the responsibility to cease sinning.

That is the epiphany of atonement ... becoming the fruit of the true vine.

Atonement could then be called the species of vine that is Jesus. The Apostles are the branches of that vine, with the fruit hanging from those branches being the sweet grapes of forgiveness, through the Salvation that comes from receiving the Holy Spirit.

Everything is possible because the true vine is alive, with all of that life beginning from one death. Jesus said that one seed must die so that it can produce many seeds ... so that many may become one with the living vine.

If you walk outside and look for a tree, you know the tree is alive because there are leaves on it ... maybe even some fruit is blossoming, budding and growing.

The concept of "tree" assumes life, and not modified by the

word "dead." It assumes all parts that make up a tree, as one, are present and functioning properly. A "tree" is one body made up of elements and parts; but all of the elements and parts are one with the living tree.

You do not look on the ground under the tree and see sticks and fallen limbs … even fallen fruit … and say, "Oh, look! A tree separated into parts … dead and alive."

We know that trees have trunks and limbs, with an internal system of cells that takes the water absorbed through the roots and sends it out through conduits and channels … a flow of sap within … to the tree's leaves, which convert sunlight into food for the tree … so the branches can produce buds of fruit.

That is how the Holy Spirit flows through the body of Christ, into all those disciples who believe in him and the Father.

If you see a fallen limb, you know it is dead wood, no longer part of the living tree. You cannot go nail a dead limb back on a tree, expecting it to spring back to life; although a branch split, while still green, can be mended back to life with the application of grafting tape.

This is why it is important to realize that all Christians **MUST** remain alive in Christ and never dry up … never stop producing fruit (if ever) … and never fall dead onto the ground.

You stay alive in Christ through love … but that requires understanding that **LOVE** is like the sap of a tree … always cursing through one's veins, within. **LOVE** is the Holy

Easter Sermons: Fifth Sunday of Easter, Year B

Spirit of God. The unique **LOVE** of a Jesus atonement vine flows because of faith in Jesus as the Son of God.

John explained this love element, saying, "we abide in him and he in us."

Jesus also said to his disciples, "Abide in me as I abide in you."

Parts and elements as **ONE** in the true living vine. **YOU** are Jesus, when Jesus is in **YOU**. When Jesus is in **YOU**, **YOU** become subservient to the Mind of Christ, allowing **YOU** to **ACT** exactly as did Jesus.

Thus, when John wrote, "Those who say, "I love God," and hate their brothers or sisters, are liars," you have to look at this as a dead branch under a tree … no longer part of the life of the whole … feeling hatred for the living branches and leaves above, jealous that it's death keeps it from that life.

A dead branch can no longer say, "The sap of life flows through me."

Nothing about being Christian is about **YOU** acting selfishly for **YOU**.

Everything about being Christian is about Christ using **YOU** as a new branch of Jesus, bearing fruit that will rejoice with the Holy Spirit, becoming **ONE** with the living vine.

Throughout every week in the Counting of the Easter Omer, you have to see how the counting of the days is towards the celebration of the First Fruits of Christ ... *Shavuot* Christians.

The Ethiopian eunuch was a ranking member of the court of Candace, the queen of the Ethiopians. Therefore, he was somebody of earthly importance.

But, he was a disciple of God ... in need of guidance as he read words on a scroll as he travelled through the wilderness of Judea.

When Philip heard him reading Scripture, Philip made the Ethiopian eunuch realize how little he knew with his brain running his body. So, he invited Philip into his chariot to guide him.

The Easter season is about going beyond being a student, being more than a disciple, and becoming **ONE** with God, through Christ and the Holy Spirit.

To get to that point, one must take some dedicated steps towards faith. You cannot just lie on the ground under the true vine, dead to the flow of the Holy Spirit's sap of life, pretending to love God, and truly expect to have someone like Philip run up ready to give you the Holy Spirit.

The Easter season is when we blossom, when we open up and ask to be pollinated in our preparation for producing fruit. The Easter season is when we demonstrate our being a strong and healthy branch ... arms of Christ reaching out to others ... not grabbing all you can for yourself.

It is your chariot you ride in. You don't have to stop for anyone in this wilderness of life in the material realm.

# Easter Sermons: Fifth Sunday of Easter, Year B

It is up to you to decide: Do you want enlightenment?

Do you want everlasting life?

Do you see a need to **ACT** for Atonement?

Do you want to volunteer to be a scapegoat for Christ?

Amen

# SIXTH SUNDAY OF EASTER

# YEAR B

**Relevant readings:**
Acts 10:44-48
Psalm 98
1 John 5:1-6
John 15:9-17

## The family and friends of Christ

The last four Sundays we have incorporated a prayer into the service that represents a counting of the Easter Omer. Today is the Sixth Sunday of the Easter Season, meaning forty-three days have passed since Our Lord was offered to the Temple as a sacrifice to God.

Easter Sermons: Sixth Sunday of Easter, Year B

Let us pray:

Today is six weeks and one day, as forty-three days towards the Omer – our measure as fruits of the Lord Jesus Christ – which culminates with our receipt of your Holy Spirit on the Day of Pentecost.

Guide us this day to learn from your words and find insight from you ... as the Word of Life ... so we may be strengthened in our devotion to God our LORD and His Holy Son, through the Holy Spirit.

Amen

Last Sunday was named Good Shepherd Sunday.

There is no special name for the sixth Sunday of the Eastertide, but a good name would be "Friends and Family Sunday."

While it is easy to grasp that from hearing Jesus tell his disciples, "I have called you friends," it may be more difficult to pick up on the family theme.

Still, that hint of family is in all of the readings today, including the Gospel of John.

Last week we read of the Apostle Philip hearing an Ethiopian eunuch reading from the scroll of Isaiah; and how Philip joined with the eunuch, to explain how Jesus of Nazareth was the one of whom Isaiah prophesied.

You have to be able to see that the Ethiopian eunuch was Jewish, which was how and why he would be reading from

Isaiah.

This is not expressly known as a clear detail from history; but many believe the place known as Beta Israel, which is located in Ethiopia, began sometime after Solomon met the Queen of Sheba. Due to Solomon's wisdom having been proved to her – through her hard questioning – she saw the wisdom of Solomon and converted to what we now call Judaism. She adopted the Mosaic Law and taught that to her people.

The Ethiopian version of what took place then says Solomon and the queen shared the gift of child, while the queen stayed in Solomon's home. The child was born after the queen returned home to Sheba.

The only point that I wish to make now – although the history of Beta Israel is very interesting story that is worth investigating further – is that Philip was able to join with the Ethiopian in his chariot **because** they were both family ... as Jews, in the sense that they both worshipped the One God Yahweh.

Acts 2 lists the names of peoples from foreign lands who had pilgrimaged to Jerusalem for *Shavuot*. Although nothing is stated about Ethiopians, they would have been there as well. The festivals represented the time when a 'family reunion' took place, with all the relatives of YHWH.

This aspect of family was stated by Jesus when he said, "I was sent only to the lost sheep of Israel." (Matthew 15:24 NIV) Those lost Israelites ... the Jews of Judah and the scattered remnants of Israel ... were the family of Jesus.

# Easter Sermons: Sixth Sunday of Easter, Year B

When Jesus was encountered by the Samaritan woman at the well, Jesus did not speak directly to her until she had spoken to him. Jesus did initiate that conversation by sending a telepathic connection with her, telling her to say to Jesus (a Jew), "Give me a drink." For Jesus to speak to a stranger, known as a Samaritan woman, would have been against the rules of the lawyers in Jerusalem. Jesus did not directly break their rule, which is understood when his disciples returned from having gone to purchase food, demanding that Jesus, "Send her away, for she keeps crying out after us."

They disciples wanted the Samaritan woman sent away because she was not family, and Jewish law forbid Jews from socializing with non-Jews ... Gentiles.

Samaritans were particularly off-limits, because they had Israelite ancestry; but their ancestors had allowed themselves to become impure by inter-breeding with their Gentile overlords.

This needs to be understood and firmly grasped, because **we** are non-Jewish ... meaning **we** do not adhere to the laws that the Jews were commanded. We do not possess a Covenant with the LORD – officially having agreed to observe ... eternally. Therefore, the Samaritan woman and **her family** have to be seen as a reflection of **us**, today.

This means – in the eyes of non-Christian Jews today – we are Gentiles; and **that** means – in the eyes of the non-Christian Jews – that we are unclean – impure – and not part of their family ... neither their religious family ... nor their racial family.

Now, in the reading from the Book of the Acts of the Apostles today, we catch a glimpse of this "non-family" problem. It whizzes by when we hear read, "The circumcised believers who had come with Peter were astounded that the gift of the Holy Spirit had been poured out <u>even on the Gentiles</u>."

The reading today comes from the very end of Acts' chapter 10, which is a wonderful story about Cornelius – a Roman centurion – a Gentile – who was told by an angel of God he met in a vision to "Send men to Joppa to bring back a man named Simon who is called Peter."

As Cornelius was obeying that command, he sent officers who were like himself – "devout and God-fearing," having given "generously to those in need and prayed to God regularly." Peter, meanwhile, was having a vision of his own, seeing unclean animals – "all kinds of four-footed animals, as well as reptiles and birds." Simon-Peter saw those creatures being brought down from heaven on something like a large, four-cornered sheet.

Peter was hungry and awaiting his lunch to be prepared when he had this vision. He saw and then heard a voice say, "Get up, Peter. Kill and eat."

Peter's response was, "Surely not, Lord! I have never eaten anything impure or unclean."

The voice then said, "Do not call anything impure that God has made clean."

At that time, the officers of Cornelius arrived in Joppa, at the place the angel said they could find Simon-Peter, and they requested to see him. Because of his vision, Peter invited Gentiles into that place he was staying. That meant Roman officers, soldiers under their Centurion, gathered together along with Peter and his Jewish followers, who were fellow believers in Jesus as Christ.

Peter then followed the Roman soldiers to the home of Cornelius, in Caesarea. There, everyone gathered with the Centurion's family and friends who followed him.

Upon greeting Peter in his home, Cornelius knelt before Peter. Peter told Cornelius to stand up because he was just a man, like Cornelius.

Then Peter said to Cornelius, "You are well aware that it is against our law for a Jew to associate with or visit a Gentile. But God has shown me that I should not call anyone impure or unclean."

Knowing this set-up, we can now see how today's reading says, "While Peter was still speaking, the Holy Spirit fell upon all who heard the word."

It was then that the Jews who accompanied Peter were

amazed at what those Gentiles began doing, because the Holy Spirit had filled them.

We read how, "They [the Jews] heard them [the Gentiles] speaking in tongues and extolling God."

The only way a Jew could know that Roman soldiers were "speaking in tongues" – in languages that were foreign to them – is because the Jews recognized those tongues.

The "tongues" that "extoll God," which praise the LORD, are the Hebrew scriptures that may be seen as written in various dialects.

Since the Psalms are specifically recognized as songs of praise to God, and since the Psalms of David were known-by-heart to those of the Jewish family – like an Adele or Taylor Swift song is known by young people today – I can imagine the astonishment expressed by the Jews visiting Cornelius' house that day was because those burly Roman soldiers were singing Psalms – in Hebrew – while being filled with the Holy Spirit.

Moreover, the Romans would have been pointing out how Scripture, including the songs of praise and the Prophets, had foretold of the coming Messiah. **AND** ... they would be singing how that foretold man was Jesus of Nazareth.

**THAT** is what happened to the disciples of Jesus, after spending an Eastertide with their Lord and Master. On the Day of Pentecost they too spoke in tongues and extolled God.

The **family** aspect then comes after Peter heard and witnessed that miracle, which caused him to say, "Can anyone withhold the water for baptizing these people who have received the Holy Spirit just as we have?"

When Peter ordered those Gentiles "to be baptized in the name of Jesus Christ," the symbol of baptism by physical water is then seen as that which denotes conversion to the form of Judaism.  The use of physical water symbolically washed their past sins all away, in recognition that the promised Messiah had indeed come to Gentiles.  By them also being born **in the name of Jesus** … as the Christ reborn into unclean flesh that had been made pure by God … everyone there was then members of a new family - **Christians**.

This means the baptism by water separated non-Christian Jews from Jewish Christians.

**It is imperative to realize** … faith in Jesus of Nazareth, as the Messiah, was not a simple act of saying, "I believe in Jesus Christ, the only Son of God."

**FAITH** in Jesus as the Son of God can only come from the enlightenment of **understanding** that comes from the Holy Spirit … where the prophecies of Jesus in the Old Testament – the Torah, the Psalms and the Prophets – bring about **UNSHAKABLE BELIEF** in that **TRUTH**.

Physical water does not bring about faith.  Faith brings about the Holy Spirit, which is the baptism that resurrects Jesus Christ in a disciple.  Physical water is then symbolic of what has already occurred.

We saw the Ethiopian eunuch filled with the Holy Spirit

first, as he heard Philip explain the meaning of Isaiah – and **then** Philip baptized him with physical water, converting that Ethiopian Jew into a Jewish Christian.

We are part of that family by our faith and belief, such that the original Covenant that binds God's chosen people to the One God, as His servants and His priests is amended to include that faith in Jesus as the Christ, as the Son of God, who was sent to lead all who believe in him to heaven.

In this way, each one of us is expected to be like those Roman soldiers and do exactly as David sang in Psalm 98:

> "Sing to the LORD a new song, for he has done marvelous things."

We each are – ourselves – a "new song," ones that "sing praises" to God because of the Holy Spirit within.

After Philip left the Ethiopian eunuch, he continued on his way, "rejoicing in the Lord." He was extolling God, just as were the Jewish followers of Peter **along with** the Roman centurions of Cornelius.

The all sang to the LORD as new song **as part of a new family** of God's servants.

Likewise, Peter and his Jewish companions, who had been forbidden from associating or visiting a Gentile, then accepted Cornelius' invitation, "to stay for several days."

Jesus and his disciples were made the same offer by the Samaritan woman and her family. Jesus took them up on their offer and "he stayed for two days." (John 4:40)

Easter Sermons: Sixth Sunday of Easter, Year B

After all, they were evidently all family in Christ then … made pure by the Holy Spirit of God.

Now, in the Gospel reading we see how Jesus told his disciples, "I have called you friends."

You have to see "friends" as the extension of family, where "friends" are those of the same "blood" but they are "friends" because they share the same religious beliefs. The disciples of Jesus were relatives, but they were closer by sharing a spiritual connection to God, through Jesus as the Christ.

The law Peter reminded Cornelius of meant, "Servants of God do not associate with those who do not believe in the LORD of our family of faith. However, God has told me not to follow an external commandment that has me avoid association with all Gentiles, because God will lead me to befriend those Gentiles who have also been purified by His Holy Spirit."

As such, we read how Jesus told his disciples (which included Peter), "You are my friends <u>if you do what I command you</u>." This is that connectivity to God, where the Holy Spirit is sent to us by belief in Christ, which then commands us to be reborn as Jesus – in our actions.

A "friend" of Jesus is then one who presents Christ to others, so that all who hear the word can be filled with the Holy Spirit … even Gentiles.

If you know the story of Cornelius and his officers who prayed to the One God and gave to those in need, you have to understand that unknowing Gentiles can **see** Christians **ACTING** and they can hear Christians TALKING ... such that the Holy Spirit can fall upon all who have ears that hear what it takes and believe the **ACTS** of Christians are the right way to be.

This is why Jesus told his disciples, "I do not call you servants any longer, because the servant does not know what the master is doing." Through the Holy Spirit a **Christ**ian instantly knows "everything that [Jesus] heard from his Father."

They know that because they too hear the Father speaking to them ... and they too **do** as the Father commands.

This naming of God as "the Father" is where we all become related, all as family, all as friends. This familial relationship is then extended through the ages, because it is as Jesus said, "I appoint you to go and bear fruit, fruit that will last."

The "fruit that lasts" is demonstrated every time someone comes to a "friend of Jesus" – an Apostle - without the lasting presence of the Holy Spirit, **but then leaves** that encounter "rejoicing in the LORD," baptized by the Holy Spirit.

Thus, as John wrote in his first open letter to all Christians – Jewish and Gentile – "Everyone who believe that Jesus is the Christ has been **born of God**; and everyone who **loves** the parent **loves** the child."

We are all family as children of God, knowing that "we love the children of God" by the way "we love God and obey his commandments."

The family of **Jews** had the Law etched on stone tablets … stored in a powerful Ark … which lore has it was stolen by the son Solomon sired with the Queen of Sheba. Stone tablets in a building, in a box, mean belief in those things is faith lost. It is lost due to those being EXTERNAL powers. It is then the presence of belief that God has been kept captive in a building.

The family of **Christians** has every law known by God written on each individual's heart – the seat of love – so obedience to those laws in never burdensome.

Christians **LOVE** doing whatever the voice of God commands … as Peter did, after his vision and conversation with God.

Jesus said to his disciples, which means he is saying to you – always – "I am giving you these commandments so that you may love one another."

You are commanded to love your family, friends, and neighbors as you love yourself, because you are all of the same blood in Christ.

Amen

# SEVENTH SUNDAY OF EASTER

# YEAR B

**Relevant readings:**
Acts 1:15-26
Psalm 1
1 John 5:9-13
John 17:6-19

## Who here among us are believers?

We have reached the seventh Sunday of the Easter Season.

In a way it is the last Sunday of Easter, as Pentecost is the bridge from Easter to the Ordinary although it falls under the Easter heading. Like *Pesach* is one festival and *Shavuot* is another, so too do Easter and Pentecost reflect.

# Easter Sermons: Seventh Sunday of Easter, Year B

The last five Sundays we have incorporated a prayer into the service that represents a counting of the Easter Omer.

Today is the Seventh Sunday, meaning a complete fifty days have passed since Our Lord was offered to the Temple as a sacrifice to God. The Covenant of Moses has been delivered from the clouds atop Mount Sinai..

However, the Christian Omer counting awaits the delivery of the Covenant written into our hearts.

Let us pray:

Today is seven weeks and one day, as fifty days towards the Omer – our measure as fruits of the Lord Jesus Christ – which culminates with our receipt of your Holy Spirit on the Day of Pentecost.

Guide us this day to learn from your words and find insight from you ... as the Word of Life ... so we may be strengthened in our devotion to God our LORD and His Holy Son, through the Holy Spirit.

Amen

Since we have reached the Fiftieth day, based on the omer of barley being taken to the Temple on the first day after the Day after the Passover (Nisan 16), the Christian count differs. The Fiftieth day should be today, but when our count is based on counting from the discovery that Jesus was resurrected from death ... 7 days into that count ... we get to add another week. Thus, next Sunday will be the Christian Pentecost.

Still, it is important to realize that next Sunday, May 24th, is the Jewish beginning of *Shavuot*. Thus, next Sunday is also their recognition of the Pentecost. So, we are all on the same page then.

The first day of the 2015 Jewish Passover was April 4th, such that the day Christians would recognize as Easter Sunday would have been April 12th, based on that starting point. However, we celebrated Easter on April 5th.

This means, in the year 2015, Christian Easter coincided with Jewish Passover (*Shabbat*, April 4 / Sunday, April 5), as does both the Jewish and Christian designation of Pentecost (*Shavuot* Pentecost May 24 / Christian Pentecost May 25).

Next year that will not be the case. Most years that is not the case.

This difference as to when a commanded observance should take place is one of several found between two religions that share a common devotion to the One God. The differences in the Judeo-Christian religions become an issue because the two only occasionally meet and share traditions now, with the rest of the time the two branches being far apart and separate.

It is important to understand that no matter how friendly Christians are with Jews, there is a deep divide between those who believe Jesus was the promised Messiah – promised to the children of Israel – and those who do **not** believe that Jesus was truly the Son of God. Most Jews still think they remain always God's chosen people.

Easter Sermons: Seventh Sunday of Easter, Year B

What is not always known by everyone is how the early Christians – both Jews and Gentiles as one – celebrated the exact same festivals as those found commanded in Leviticus. Jews and early Christians always celebrated the same festivals on the same days. The early Christians, who were predominately of Jewish lineage, never called the day of Jesus' resurrection "Easter."

It was this way for nearly four hundred years.

Today, we see how that constant has been changed … modified to attract more Gentiles, those who had similar festivals around the same times of year.

The name "Easter" comes from pagan roots, as a similar name, one used to mark a spring festival that belonged to a Proto-Indo-European goddess of fertility. She also was a representative of the dawn.

Awareness of this history of change and adjustment is important because it models the changes and adjustments that took place in the Kingdom of Israel, under Solomon (at first), which led to a split into Israel and Judah, then the loss of everything God had promised them.

The promise was based on conditions **not** being changed and adjusted.

But as the saying goes, "Give them an inch and they will take a mile."

I remind you of all of this because in the Gospel reading today from John. Jesus was heard to pray to God, asking for God's help with those who would take Jesus' place – the early Christians.

In that prayer, Jesus said, "I am not asking on behalf of the world, but on behalf of those whom you gave me."

When you hear those words in that prayer, knowing that Jesus was a Jew and all of his disciples were also Jews, you realize Jesus was not asking God to make everyone in the world a Christian.

In Jesus' prayer, he was not setting expectations like an emperor who expected to conquer a part of the world and put up signs saying, "Everyone must now consider themselves the nationality of the Emperor." The Roman, Greek, English and every empire asks their god(s) to help make all the rebels comply with the will of their overlords.

Jesus was **not** asking God to help him decide what pagan festivals would best coincide with Jewish festivals, to make integrating people easier, so those who believed in many gods could change and adjust to believing in just one. Christianity is not designed to work that way.

We see that when we read how Jesus prayed, "I have made your name known to those whom you gave me from the world. They were yours, and you gave them to me, and they have kept your word."

Think about those words for a moment.

<pause>

Jesus was given **Jews** as disciples, because those Jews were God's people **AND** those Jewish disciples "had kept God's word," having taken God's laws to heart.

Now in those words in that prayer, Jesus does not name the Jews of the world specifically as being a limitation on who God **could** give him. By not saying that, this prayer not only allows one to see Jesus praying for God to help his disciples and followers then – 2000 years ago – but it allows that prayer to extend from the day it was spoken to now, this very day ... and beyond.

We are of the world now, and **if** we are devoted to serving God, as shown by us keeping His word, **then** we can be given by God to Jesus – as true Christians.

This means it is important to realize that when Jesus prayed, "I am not asking on behalf of the world," this relates to the message we heard two weeks ago, from the first epistle of John, which stated, "Those who say, "I love God," and hate their brothers and sisters, are liars."

Those "who say "I love God," and hate their "brothers and sisters" were the Jews of Jesus' and John's day, those related through a devotion to their religion. Jews then "hated" the Jews who believed Jesus of Nazareth was the Messiah. They persecuted them, stoning them to death ... crucifying them.

This means that Jesus was not praying for God to help the whole world, with all of its Jewish descendants, whose blood could make them believe they were God's chosen people, with a birthright of favor. Instead, Jesus was praying for those who truly were priests, who desired to serve God through their faith that Jesus was indeed the Messiah ... the Son of God.

This is important to grasp, because **if** Jesus was **not** praying for God to help the whole world, and **not** for God to help the Jews who hated Christians, **then** Jesus was praying **only** for true Christians – those who **he** would fill with God's Holy Spirit ... and no one else.

Now, in the story from the Book of the Acts of the Apostles we read about the selection of Matthias to be one of a group of twelve. On the day before Pentecost, after the Ascension of Jesus, we see how "Peter stood up with the Eleven, raised his voice and addressed the crowd."

Matthias filled the position that was vacated by Judas' betrayal of Jesus and his subsequent suicide, which reduced the disciple 'executive board' from twelve to eleven. Because Jesus had many more followers and close supporters than twelve (many were family relations), the naming of twelve is an organizational step. Still, it means twelve is significant and with purpose.

The number twelve is a sacred number ... a symbolic number, meaning that it was important to take the number that had been reduced to eleven back to twelve. Numerologically (a tool some of the Jews understood), twelve is a base three (1+2=3), where three reflects an initial completion of solid steps taken. Twelve is a statement of higher completion, which has divine connotations. Therefore, twelve lead disciples (i.e.: supervisors) made Jesus' ministry more than a gang of thirteen.

Now, both numbers – 11 and 12 – have mystical meaning that requires some study, and I recommend everyone look deeper into the symbolism of each number, 11 and 12, as both reflect a choice to become elevated spiritually, while still on the physical plane.

However, it is more important to focus your minds now on the Acts reading, as to who was capable of filling that vacant position. Besides looking at the two candidates to fill the opening, one should look as well at who is **never** allowed to be considered for such a role of responsibility.

The reading today begins by stating, "Peter stood up among the believers (together the crowd numbered about one hundred twenty persons)."

This "election" to fill a position on the "high counsel" of the earliest state of Christianity's Church took place on the forty-ninth day in the Jewish counting of the omer. That day was the Seventh **Sabbath** from the Passover (also a Sabbath) – the day before Pentecost (a Sunday). the next day (unbeknownst to them then) would be when "all of them were filled with the Holy Spirit and began to speak in other tongues."

It is important to see "the believers" as being disciples of Jesus, because Peter said the choice had to come "of the men who have accompanied us during all the time that the Lord Jesus went in and out among us, beginning from the baptism of John until the day he was taken up from us."

The forty-ninth day was when Lord Jesus was "taken up," meaning the Ascension took place on a most holy **Sabbath**. The forty days prior to that Ascension was when "about one hundred twenty" believers (who had all assisted in Jesus' ministry) - learned from their Lord for three years - they too spent their time with the risen Jesus.

As such, Peter could then say, "one of these **must** become a witness with us to his resurrection." One of those had to rise and become the twelfth man at the table of Christ.

Jesus did not just appear risen and spend forty days with only eleven disciples. He appeared and taught one hundred twenty disciples for forty days, with eleven of those being his "inner circle," with one position there vacant.

You might note that "about one hundred twenty" is **ten times** 'about twelve'. With Judas missing, the "number of persons" among who Peter stood to address might well have been 121, so that when one of that number was selected to become one of the twelve, there were then twelve counsel disciples and ten times twelve priestly disciples.

There is that number twelve again … just not as clearly stated.

The point to grasp firmly here is Peter addressed "**believers**" of Jesus as the Christ, who had witnessed the *Rabbouni* Jesus, the trial and death of the man Jesus, and the risen Lord Jesus, as well as his Ascension. The "**believers**" had dedicated the past three years of their lives to reach that point of being called "**believers**."

Thus, when it came time to select a "high counsel" disciple to replace Judas, they didn't run an ad in the Jerusalem Gazette, saying, "Professional organizer needed. Must be Jewish and have good people skills. Apply in the city where a man carrying a jar of water will meet you and lead you to an upstairs room."

# Easter Sermons: Seventh Sunday of Easter, Year B

Peter was not seeking a replacement for Judas "from the world" of Jews.

To use an analogy from athletics, in particular football – where injuries are most frequent and replacements are always needed – they have the "next man up" philosophy.

This means that when a starting player is injured and cannot play, the coach does not ask for the microphone and then address the spectators, announcing, "Anyone who thinks he or she can play quarterback, please go to the equipment room now and put on a uniform." Instead, a reserve player is already dressed, already trained in the playbook, and ready, willing, and eagerly able to get on the field of play.

This same philosophy filled the early Christian Church, and it was repeated all through Jesus' prayer to God, stated as "I have made your name known to those," "they have kept your word," "protect them in your name," "so that they may have my joy made complete in themselves," and "so that they may be sanctified in truth."

"They" was not a third person pronoun that could apply generally to the whole world. It referred to Jesus' team of disciples and on-field assistants.

Jesus prayed to God about his "team of players," who had been coached, trained, practiced, and prepared to "get in the game" of priesthood, when game day came.

John remembered Jesus saying that prayer soon before he was arrested and turned over to the Temple as the sacrificial lamb – the first day in the counting of the omer.

John also recalled (although it is not read today) how Jesus not only prayed for the disciples numbering "about one hundred twenty persons," but for others coming later. Jesus prayed, "My prayer is not for them alone. I pray also for those who will believe in me through their message."

We are "those who will believe in Jesus through the message" of all the earliest Christians.

This means that just like the disciples Peter stood up before, in order to choose one who would become one of the hierarchical replacements of the Church of Christ, **ALL** candidates - **all members of the Church** - must be seasoned, trained, and vested in their **belief** that Jesus was the Son of God.

That means you are either on the team or you are **not** on the team; and even though there are many more fans of a team than there are team members, a fan is **not** on the team.

Now, anyone who has sat at this bus stop before and heard me preach for any length of time has probably heard me refer to the "big brain syndrome." Let me explain that once more.

We live in an age when intellect is king. We see ourselves – as Americans – as the latest, greatest, smartest human beings ever to be a part of this world. Many American Christians have read the Bible and even studied what others have written to explain all about the Bible, but therein comes a flaw. Instead of Christ as our King, we let our big brain rule over us.

Easter Sermons: Seventh Sunday of Easter, Year B

With a big brain, and when one reads the Bible after 2000 years of "thinking about all that," one immediately begins identifying with God, with Jesus, with the Apostles, and with all the "good guys" – prophets and Patriarchs. That identification is because our big brains tell us, "I have **heard** how the story goes. Since I have **studied** some things, that confirms that I am a fan of their team."

The problem that comes when one contracts "big brain syndrome" is one becomes blind to just how much one needs to see the **need** for the Holy Bible to be read as a warning **not** to allow yourself to become the villain in the story. To fully understand that **need**, one has to **know** where the villains are coming from. Until you realize that **need**, <u>**you**</u> reflect the problem... not the solution.

**You** are the dreaded Pharisee that Jesus spoke to. **You** are the lame beggar who could do nothing for himself. **You** are the one filled with demons that need to be exorcized. **You** are the Romans who sentenced Jesus to death, flogged him, nailed him to a tree, and pierced his side with a spear.

**You** are part of the world that Jesus did **not** pray to God to help become priests, **if** you **do not do** what it takes to truly be a **believer** that Jesus was prophesied by the prophets, foretold in the psalms of David, and predicted in the books of Moses.

The way to see the reading today from the Acts of the Apostles is with **you** being Judas Iscariot, who turned Jesus over for silver, committed suicide and lost his position of pride. You <u>**are**</u> he "who became a guide for those who arrested Jesus," even though Judas was "numbered among us and was allotted his share in this ministry," as Peter stated.

**If** you call yourself a **believer** – a Christian – **but** you do nothing to show love to your brothers and sisters in Christ, you do nothing to spread the word of Jesus to the children you influence, you are the other guy.

Instead of love, you hate certain members of a church that you do not think are true Christians. They, of course, are the ones who you are too afraid to confront directly, preferring more than talk behind their backs – never to their face. Every time you act in this way, **you betray** Jesus Christ.

Today, in John's first epistle, we heard him echoing those remarks he made two weeks back, saying:

> "Those who do not believe in God have made Jesus a liar by not believing in the testimony that God has given concerning his Son."

That testimony today is "**believe** in Jesus Christ and receive the Holy Spirit, by becoming a holy priest – a saint – in the commission of the Church of Christ," where eternal spiritual life is the reward from a sacrificed physical life.

Judas heard those promises, but he kept his hand on the purse of the church. He loved the feel of money … the power of gold and riches. Judas was also considered to be an "intellectual, " a "thinking man," who loved to pick Jesus' brain.

As such, Judas could not see beyond the material plane, to the heavenly plane, so he wasted his time alive in this realm plotting and **thinking** about how he could get ahead. Judas spent his time **thinking** he was as smart as Jesus. Judas thought his brain was as good as - if not better than - the Mind of Christ, which came to Jesus through the Holy Spirit of God. It was the Mind of Christ, not a big brain that allotted Jesus that grace.

If only Judas' big brain hadn't gotten in his way.

As John wrote, "If we receive human testimony, the testimony of God is greater."

Think about that for one moment.

<pause>

Everything written about Scripture that is not divine is "human testimony." To read Scripture as if mere human beings used their big brains to recount history, tell stories they were not witnesses to personally, or prophesy and/or write prophetic songs, is to receive "human testimony." For the books of the Holy Bible to be read as truly "the testimony of God," one needs to set the big brain aside and pray, "God help me understand the full truth of these words."

Trying to memorize the English translations of Bible verses is hard enough (given the lack of time most Christians spend reading the Holy Bible); but add in reading all the great biblical philosophers who added their two cents. It is enough for one's big brain to want to explode.

When one is spiritually led to divine insight, there is no brain freeze, as the truth comes from the source, as "the testimony of God." That certainly is greater than the biggest brain.

Today is Sunday, a day Christians see as when God rested. Rather than the Sabbath (a Saturday), we believe Sunday is when God changed and adjusted his commandments about when the Sabbath should be remembered and kept holy.

But on this day of rest and holiness, how many will leave here today and go the next six days, twenty hours and however many minutes **not** spending more than a few fleeting moments in prayer?

How much time will be spent in reflection on the Scriptures?

Other than the hired hand that wears a robe and cross and orates behind podiums above altars or the guy like me, who wears jeans and sneakers while talking at bus stops, who else will leave here today and put a lot of effort into living as a priest in a ministry for Jesus Christ?

It is our big brains that keep the Holy Spirit from coming into us. Our mental disease keeps God out of our hearts and Christ away from our minds. Without that presence, there is nothing holy about our life's direction.

Next Sunday is the Day of Pentecost, when the one hundred twenty disciples of Jesus became Apostles and spread the Holy Spirit to the world. That spread would be to those who would first **believe** ... through their readiness and practice ...leading them to take actions based on faith.

The Easter Season ... these past seven weeks ... have been counting down the days until **we** should be filled with the Holy Spirit. For forty-nine days **we should have been seeking the risen Lord Jesus** to show **us** the proof we

Easter Sermons: Seventh Sunday of Easter, Year B

<u>need</u> to lay our big brains aside and receive the Spirit.

Are we ready?

Have we done our preparations?

Are we ready for the call: **"NEXT MAN UP!"**

Amen

# PENTECOST SUNDAY

# YEAR B

**Relevant readings:**
Acts 2:1-21 or
Ezekiel 37:1-14
Psalm 104:24-34 & 35b
Romans 8:22-27 or
Acts 2:1-21
John 15:26-27 and
John 16:4b-15

## Prophesying to dried bones

The Counting of the Easter Omer is over. We have reached *Shavuot* – the Festival of Weeks – traditionally representative of when the First Fruits of the harvest would be turned over to the priests if the temple, to be sacrificed on the altar.

Over the past seven Sundays, we have heard Jesus refer to the fruit of the true vine; and today is when we read of how the disciples became living fruit of the Jesus vine, speaking in the tongues of many lands.

Because the true vine still lives and still produces fruit, I welcome those who have regularly sat at this bus stop over the past Eastertide, patiently waiting for their bus to arrive and take them to a more important place than this. I welcome those to now stand and speak in the language of Scripture, telling the others here why they should believe he or she is a fruit of the true vine.

\<pause\>

\<cue "crickets chirping" sound-bite\>

Well, that silence speaks louder than words.

I imagine if Ezekiel had been a bus stop preacher, he might have heard God ask, "Mortal, can any of those dried bones on the bus stop bench stand on its own and speak?"

Ezekiel's answer would still be applicable: "O Lord GOD, you know."

Sorry to put strangers on the spot, asking for volunteers to speak in tongues on Pentecost Sunday, but there is solace to be found in knowing dried bones can find life. If slow-witted disciples can become Apostles, and people from all nations can understand multiple foreign languages coming from Galilean rubes, then life can come to dried bones when they receive the Holy Spirit.

The first step in that direction is accomplished by willingly reading a sermon - any sermon - but preferably one that is longer than a 50-word blog. You have accomplished that ... **if** you willingly finish reading this sermon.

The next step is to realize a sermon is **not** anything more than one person's thoughts and feelings about Scripture. When you realize that anyone can write a sermon – simply by reading something in the Holy Bible, taking the time to think about it (pray about it), and then placing those thoughts on paper – the point is not so much the words but the impact those words have on people. Writing a composition about "What I **think** Scripture says" is not going to fill anyone with the Holy Spirit.

But not speaking your words aloud to an audience or not making them available for others to read online means your ideas are not really a sermon. That is more akin to self-justification.

Have you ever thought about Scripture while you were away from a place that regularly and formally requires your mind to ponder Christian issues ... like a church does?

Have you had scriptural insights at the work place, or while playing sports?

Do you regularly speak to God like you believe He is listening?

Have you ever pondered questions that came to you about what something in Scripture meant, to the point of being motivated to look that up online - or personally ask someone to answer that question – someone you think to be more knowledgeable of Christian studies than you are?

Have you taken the step to regularly attend Bible Studies or extracurricular – voluntary – classes at church?

Have you ever volunteered to lead a class of that nature?

Are you still doing all of the above: Taking your religion home with you - to work and play with you; seeking to learn more about the meaning of Scripture; entering into honest debate about how moving Scripture can be; taking the time to teach others about what you see and how your religion is relevant in how you lead your life?

Until you have answered "Yes" to all these questions, you cannot expect that God does **not** to see your **lack** of effort, your **fear** of taking a leap of faith, and your **selfish** views of religion. The way you act speaks loudly as an indication of whether **you** want God's help ... or not.

God is not withholding His Holy Spirit from you, **YOU** are refusing to receive what God offers, through true faith in Jesus Christ.

In the Gospel reading from John, Jesus is remembered to have said, "When [God] comes" – meaning when God comes to **you** – "[God] will prove the world wrong about sin and righteousness and judgment."

Now, Jesus went on to explain the meaning of that, but before we go over what Jesus said, do **you** – as part of the world - have **any** idea or opinion about what **sin** is?

Robert Tippett

Can you explain what **righteousness** is?

Do you understand the concept of **judgement**?

If you <u>think</u>, then of course you have ideas about the meaning of each.

And, it is okay to venture the most wild guesses at this point, because you have all (basically, through silence) already admitted you are clueless about what being filled with the Holy Spirit is like. That means **you** are in that blissful state of ignorance, **before** God comes to **you**.

Whatever you <u>think</u> (as part of the world), God will prove you wrong.

Today, it seems our society struggles with calling some sins a **sin** at all. We read how Jesus said, "Let you without sin throw the first stone." Most normal people would hear Jesus say that and realize, "Wow! I sin every day."

In today's world, there are plenty who would say that Jesus said, "I wouldn't want to be stoned to death." That means doing away with all forms of punishment mandated by laws.

We then **think**, "Hey, if so many people are doing the same wrong things I am doing ... and since so many who are doing them also call themselves believers in God, as Christians, then who am I to say something is a sin?"

Make everything legal and no one breaks the law!

Easter Sermons: Pentecost Sunday, Year B

We like to think of God as the mean ogre of the Old Testament, who so often said, "Off with their heads!" Then we then like to think of Jesus as the "new wave" hippie dude, who goes around saying, "Peace man. Like ... love one another dude. That's all you gotta do man."

Do you **think** God sent his Son Jesus to say, "It is okay to sin. You are forgiven of anything and everything"?

Keep in mind how God tossed Adam and Eve out of Eden, simply because they ate forbidden fruit. Forget about that fruit having the seeds of Big Brain Syndrome and just see the fruit being sin ... of any kind. God threw His Son out of heaven because he broke a law.

As to **righteousness**, we tend to think icons are those who are righteous, such as the pope ... but I forget ... is there one or two popes? Or, is it up to three popes now? Forget him, that's a poor example.

How about our political leaders as examples of righteousness ... like President Barack Obama, or President George Bush, or President Bill Clinton and presidential hopefuls Hillary Clinton and Jeb Bush? [This was written before Donald Trump entered the foray; but add his name too.]

Well, maybe politics is not the road to righteousness. So maybe it is your priest, as to whom you look for where you find righteousness in a human?

Maybe the woman Presiding Bishop of the Episcopal Church represents righteousness?

Maybe the professors at seminary schools are righteous,

teaching priests to also be righteous?

Maybe ....

In the movie *Farris Beuller's Day Off*, the principal's assistant said, "They think Farris is a righteous dude."

Was he? Or, was that misuse of the word "righteous"?

Do we truly understand what "righteous" means?

That question then leads to the issue of **judgment**, which, today at least, is not as much a legal issue as it is more of a "die and go to heaven" issue. We are talking about Judgement Day stuff now.

What do you think is the key to getting in heaven when you die?

After all, we are all mortals and can only live for so long. So, what is **your** opinion about heaven and hell?

Who goes to the big house in the sky and who burns in the fiery pits below?

Some people may think Jesus was only talking about the way the world was in 33 A.D.

A sinner, to the Jews of his day, was anyone who broke the laws of Moses; but, as we read from week to week - how some Jews saw Jews who were lame, sick, diseased, blind, and poor as being punished by God ... for having sinned. They thought a sinner was clearly **marked** by sin; so can everyone clearly see what sin looks like on a human being?

# Easter Sermons: Pentecost Sunday, Year B

When the blind man was healed by Jesus the disciples asked Jesus, "Whose sins made that man blind? Himself or his parents?"

The Jews thought "sin" was a reflection upon the way one was seen by the society as a whole. The ones who were imperfect were deemed sinners.

Then there were the Gentiles ... especially those rascally Samaritans. They were sinners because they did not know **how** to recognize sin. They looked in the mirror and only saw a Samaritan staring back ... not a sinner.

This means, to the Jews, "sin" was the way of life for EVERYONE who did not memorize the Law ... and look good while doing it.

In Jesus' day, the righteous were thought to be those who looked good ... those who had land, title, possessions, money, position, power, and the respect of listeners, those who they stood before - the gathered crowds seeking guidance. The righteous were thought to be those who were especially versed in the laws of Moses, the stories of the Torah, the lyrics of the psalms, and the writings of the prophets.

Righteousness was then seen as relative to how much religion one knew. How much time one spent learning those important details meant one spent time not sinning, simply by studying holy books.

Based on all that, judgment was one of those things the so-called righteous didn't believe came after mortal death. Most of the religious scholars in the Temple did not believe in *Sheol* (Hell), and none of them thought anyone would ever go to heaven without a proper guide. That had to wait until the Messiah came. Then, heaven would be brought to everyone back to life on earth ... for the Jews, at least.

So back then judgement was a legal issue ... as far as the Jews were concerned. If you broke the Law, you were judged.

Therefore, it might be easy to think how wrong those ancient Jews were ... about sin, righteousness and judgment ... from where we sit today. But it is just as easy to think we – our Christian society – are just as wrong **IF WE ARE NOT LED BY THE HOLY SPIRIT**.

They were **not** ... before Christ, before God's Holy Spirit was Advocated by Christ; **BUT** are we not - as a whole, as a Christian nation - **just as lifeless** as they were?

Consider this: Sin is such a struggle **before** God comes, it seems impossible not to break some rule, do some sin. However, **after** one is filled with the Holy Spirit, then sin is the last thing on one's mind.

Sin doesn't evaporate and cease to exist then. In fact, it attacks you, tries to entice you, trick you, and make you think one little sin is okay. If you still resist all the lures, it then comes after you with persecution, with crowds of people holding protest signs in front of you, calling you names, seeking Federal indictments and punishments for refusing to recognize it is our right to sin – even though sin is something you have no use for.

After God comes to **you**, you realize righteousness is God.

Easter Sermons: Pentecost Sunday, Year B

Jesus was righteous **because** God led his life and the Holy Spirit within would not permit him to fall for sin's tricks. Jesus said, "Get thee behind me, Satan!"

**You** too **must become** a temple in which God resides ... just like Jesus. **You** must protect that presence; and the actions of that protection make **you** appear righteous ... but righteousness is really God.

Judgement is then your decision to allow – welcome, request, desire – God to come into you and stay with you forever ... **BEFORE** ... all other judgments are God's to make for you ... and you willingly submit to God's will.

It is impossible for anyone to fully grasp this when someone else is telling it to them.

Everything I say now is just made-up stuff to **you** ... until **you** experience God. **Then** everything you thought about sin, righteousness and judgment changes.

The excuses ... the crutches of lameness ... which is why you cannot stand up and address the gathered crowd on the Day of Pentecost ... they get tossed away. You are healed!

In the name of Jesus Christ of Nazareth, **talk**!

At that time, you cannot stop from speaking, and you cannot say the wrong thing.

You speak the truth ...

and the truth is impressive.

The truth is attractive, leading others to you.

In the reading from Acts today, Peter stood before the gathered crowd and explained how the amazing abilities of the disciples ... those abilities with foreign languages ... was like the prophet Joel had written.

Joel wrote, "In the last days it will be, God declares, that I [God] will pour out my Spirit upon all flesh."

God said, "Your sons and your daughters shall prophesy."

"Prophecy" **IS** everything that is Scripture.

In the <u>last days of not knowing what Scripture means</u>, every iota of one's body – all flesh – will be filled with God's Spirit and then one will know everything God meant when he had a prophet write something. EVERYTHING leads one to see how Jesus Christ would be sent to save dried bones from eternal death ... giving us the **opportunity** of eternal life!

Jesus had to die for us to have that gift be given to us, as Jesus said in John's Gospel.

When Jesus died, Joel's prophecy was fulfilled ... when "The sun shall be turned to darkness."

We read how the sun went dark between the sixth hour and the ninth hour, in three of the four Gospels.

Thus, after that event, "Then everyone who calls upon the name of the Lord shall be saved."

Easter Sermons: Pentecost Sunday, Year B

You are saved by the Holy Spirit coming upon you, as advocated by Jesus Christ, when sin, righteousness and judgment are finally realized.

Sin can only be seen when one hangs out at the fringes of the law, feeling restricted by commandments written down on paper and nailed to signs along the road. Being so close to sin makes one desire sin ... and when sin whispers, "Jesus will forgive you," what happens next?

AFTER the Holy Spirit comes, the law ceases to be an external document. It becomes **your** personal way of life. You stay so far away from the boundaries of the external law that there is no distraction. Sin is always behind you because you believe in Jesus as your Messiah.

AFTER the Holy Spirit comes, righteousness is not some public figure ... like Jesus, like Peter, like Ezekiel, like someone other than **you**. **You** become like all those who were truly righteous, because those who are truly righteous have God's Spirit within. Righteousness never promotes self, but always praises God.

AFTER the Holy Spirit comes, judgment has been made. What was dead - as they say in prison lingo, "Dead man walking" - has then come to life. Judgment is acceptance of the new life that is filled with the breath of God's Holy Spirit. Judgement is the sacrifice of one's dried bones for the opportunity of other dried bones also finding new life.

In the reading for today from Ezekiel, God told Ezekiel to "Prophesy to these bones" ... and he did ... making all the bones come together and have new muscles and skin ...

**But** … prophesying to dried bones was like preaching to people who are afraid to receive the Holy Spirit …they have no life of true value ... even if they look like they are alive, they are still dead.

So, Ezekiel was told to prophesy to **the breath** … the breath of God that will bring the life of the Holy Spirit within.

When Ezekiel did that, the winds came ... just like told of in Acts on the Day of Pentecost.

Today is the Day of Pentecost and before me is a valley of dried bone.

God is calling for more sons and daughters to take the leap of faith.

When will your "last days" lead you to stand and prophesy?

Amen

Easter Sermons: Pentecost Sunday, Year B

# EASTER SERMONS

# YEAR C

# EASTER SUNDAY

# YEAR C

**Relevant readings:**
Acts 10:34-43 or
Isaiah 65:17-25
Psalm 118:1-2 & 14-24
1 Corinthians 15:19-26
or Acts 10:34-43
John 20:1-18 or
Luke 24:1-12

## The Easter hunt for resurrection

Happy Easter, bus riders! Today, instead of passing a basket for you to cover the bottom with green paper, we

# Easter Sermons: Easter Sunday, Year C

are giving out baskets with a bed of green plastic shreds, so you can hunt for the Easter eggs and the prize chocolate bunny!

I'm sorry we have no live chicks, dyed pink and yellow, and no dyed blue baby bunnies to give away. The Health Department stopped that when America became a bus stop nation and stopped being rural. There is no longer adequate space for most families to raise farm animals.

<pause>

I'm being facetious.

You see, Easter has become synonymous with the advent of spring, which symbolizes births, babies, and reproduction. Spring is when things start to grow again! A drab, barren landscape becomes a burst of colors to behold.

To celebrate the newness of spring, the Church of Rome has used its holy slide-rule and determined that Easter is the closest Sunday to the first full moon after the Vernal Equinox. The Vernal Equinox is the official timing of the season of spring.

Unfortunately, God must have forgotten to tell Moses how to calculate when the first month of the Hebrew year would be, because one would think the Moses way (as seen in all Hebrew calendars) is wrong. That means Rome had to figure out how to calculate when Easter will be each year, so its faithful would not be lost and confused.

Somehow, Rome missed how Nisan (the first month of a Hebrew year, even though it is a spring month) will always begin on the first **new** moon after the beginning of spring (the Vernal Equinox). That means 15 Nisan is when the first full moon will follow that **new** moon. Since the moon makes a complete cycle in 28 days, half of 28 is 14; so, if you add 14 days to 1 Nisan, then you get 15 Nisan.

That date signifies the beginning of Passover recognition. Passover is a God-commanded eight-day celebration, recognizing how God freed the Israelites from bondage, by sending Moses.

[**Aside**: The *Beatles* wrote a song named "Eight Days a Week," and nobody knew what that meant. An eight-day week is one that begins and ends on the same day of the week.]

In case you dropped your complimentary Easter calendars, 1 Nisan this year will be on April 7. That is when the first new moon takes place, after the official beginning of spring, which was Sunday, March 20 [2016]. So, the Jewish recognition of the Passover will be between 6:00 PM April 22 and April 30 (or 15 Nisan to 22 Nisan). Thus (and the Eastern Orthodox Church follows this method), Easter Sunday is really supposed to be May 1 this year.

But here we are, Easter basket in hand, all dressed up in our new Easter dresses, bonnets and handsome suits. So, let's make the most of a new spring having been sprung!

God did not accidentally free His chosen people after the advent of longer days in the Northern Hemisphere. It didn't just happen to be spring when Moses parted the Red Sea. God does nothing in a haphazard way.

# Easter Sermons: Easter Sunday, Year C

Spring represents the time of rebirth, when dormant plants spring back to life and renew a cycle of growth and development that produces new fruits. However, springtime in the wilderness does not mean new foods abound, from which all the Israelites could be fed.

Besides a flock of quail being flown in once to feed the group, for the Israelites led by Moses it was forty years of manna in the morning, manna in the evening, and manna at supper time. That was spring, summer, fall and winter every year.

[**Aside**: The Israelites actually had all their animals in tow with them, so they did have milk, cheese, eggs, and the occasional mutton available for their hunger needs. Manna was their Spiritual food they so vitally needed.]

Therefore, God sent Moses to lead the Israelites to a new **religious spring**, following his arrival to begin that process. Moses arrived as winter came to a close and spring had sprung upon Egypt. Once freed into the wilderness, God's chosen Israelites would be tended by the Most High Gardener, throughout all seasons.

Moses would preserve the seed in the wilderness, Joshua would sow it in Canaan, David would raise and maintain fields of crops in Israel, which would grow to eventually become Christianity.

The Israelite seed would be planted in the fertile ground of Canaan, when the timing was right. That timing was again the Passover, during Nisan, fifteen days after the first **new** moon of spring.

Knowing this, one can see how God wants his priests to offer to the world the **newness** of Spirituality. Israel was planted to become a living vine, from which priests for the One true God could be harvested, so the whole world could be fed salvation.

One can see how Jesus died and was resurrected as a spring forward from that foundation of faith ... as part of God's overall master plan.

Thus, the connection to spring and babies being born is how we think hunting for dyed eggs and bringing home a new pet for our children to experience first-hand the cycle of life is synonymous with Easter. We think birth and renewal is connected to the Resurrection of Jesus.

However, as unfortunate as it might seem ... that concept is wrong.

The rites of spring, eggs, fruit, and the quick reproductive natures of rabbits and chickens are rooted in pagan ideologies. While that can be seen to symbolize rebirth, it is only on the earthly plane. Rebirth into a mortal existence means being born into a life that leads to an assured death. Death is symbolized by the return of winter, after the fall. This is opposite how spring is a return to mortal life, that opens up fully in the summer.

In Greek mythology, the season changes are explained in the tale of Persephone, the daughter of Demeter (the earth goddess) who married Hades (god of the underworld). Hades took his new bride to his inner world, from which even gods could not escape. After Demeter refused to let new growth come upon her earth out of sadness for the loss of her daughter, an arrangement was made so Persephone could split her time with her mother on the earth, and with her husband in the underworld. When Persephone returned to the earth, Demeter had everything grow anew; but the sadness created by Persephone's returning underground led Demeter to cause the earth to morn and stop growing. This means spring, and a return to the living, merely reflects a rebirth in the same way as does reincarnation.

Reincarnation is the rebirth of an eternal soul into the eventual death of a mortal body. It is not born into eternal life because a physical body is limited to how long it can live. While Persephone reflects the changing states of a physical realm, where birth and death are always followed by renewal of a repeating cycle, Jesus' resurrection is about rebirth of a soul into the spiritual body that encompasses eternal life.

To grasp this difference, look at the mandatory reading from chapter ten of the Acts of the Apostles. Peter (who would become the adopted patron Saint of the Church of Rome) said to Cornelius and the other Roman Gentiles, "I truly understand that God shows no partiality, but in every nation anyone who fears him and does what is right is acceptable to him."

That was not spoken to a group of Roman soldiers as if Peter had a revelation that the pagan worship of spring and fertility rites - which the Romans recognized - was equivalent to "a fear of the One true God and doing what is right and acceptable to that One true God."

All humanity born to death sees no favor from God, as being born into death is a cycle of nature that God deemed to be good ... for His material creation. However, God seeded His religion into the world - through Adam and wife - so that natural cycle could find a spiritual outlet to eternal peace.

What we do not read today is how Cornelius was visited by an angel, sent by the One true God, because "[Cornelius] and all his family were devout and God-fearing; he gave generously to those in need and prayed to God regularly."

The angel instructed Cornelius to send for Simon Peter, so Jews and Gentiles could come together as one. Prior to that, Jews represented the priests-in-training for presenting salvation to the world, while the Gentiles represented the cycle of nature - birth to a world of sin, followed by death and repeat.

That is what Peter meant when he spoke of fear and doing right, which are heard in his words we read today to Cornelius. "Doing what is right," from a "fear of God," means ceasing to sin.

Jews and Gentiles alike are all welcomed by the One true God to serve only Him, with an equal reward offered to both groups of human beings ... that of being filled with God's Holy Spirit. Through the Holy Spirit, one can defeat sin (thus death), ceasing the need for repeating the cycle of reincarnation.

So, when our reading today ends by saying, "All the prophets testify about [Jesus] that everyone who believes in [Jesus] receives forgiveness of sins through [Jesus'] name," we miss where Acts 10:44-46 states:

# Easter Sermons: Easter Sunday, Year C

> "While Peter was still speaking these words, the Holy Spirit came on all who heard the message. The circumcised believers who had come with Peter were astonished that the gift of the Holy Spirit had been poured out even on Gentiles. For they heard them speaking in tongues and praising God."

Cornelius and his soldiers (who were fearful of the One true God, were generous, and were those who prayed daily) received forgiveness of sins, just as Peter and his fellow apostles had been forgiven of sins – through receipt of the Holy Spirit. All had gained the reward of eternal life, through that presence within them.

Receipt of the Holy Spirit made them all be resurrected – instantly – as a new Jesus, no longer common souls trapped in flesh that was only ensured a future death. They were reborn souls that had been washed clean of sins forever, receiving eternal salvation. Each became another Son of Man, as all were resurrections of Jesus as Sons of God.

In the reading from 1 Corinthians (an option along with Isaiah 65:17-25), Paul is shown to say:

> "**If** for this life **only** we have hoped in Christ, [**then**] we are of all people **most** to be pitied."

Think about that for a moment.

<pause>

That says (in a paraphrase):

> "**If** you worship Christ as if the Holy Spirit will magi-

cally renew your flesh, so you can enjoy the fruits of this life … **and not care about eternal life** …[**then**] you are to be pitied **more** than some pagan who worships the sun's return to being overhead longer, so the days are warmer, and so fruits and grains can grow again … but … who knows nothing about fearing the One true God."

If you do lip service to Jesus, but bow down before the Easter Bunny, then shame on you!

Anyone who knows that God offers eternal life with Him in Heaven, for a price that requires the sacrifice of self, that is an offer that should be accepted. To know that and then think: "You know what? I'm good. Rather than sacrifice my own ego, can I just get some gifts for saying I believe that eternal life thing can be done?"

A person like that needs to be pitied, just as Judas needed to be pitied for his betrayal.

Paul then went on to explain: "Since death came through a human being, the resurrection of the dead has also come through a human being."

That means everything about your human state of being – flesh, bones, and blood – is only temporarily "first fruits." Jesus of Nazareth had to be born to death, just like all human beings, as a model for all subsequent fruit of the vine.

Just like fruit – which changes from buds, to blooms, to petal fall, to fruit set, to ripe state, to fruit fall from the tree to be consumed by living creatures leaving only a pit or seed behind, from which a new tree is grown that will reproduce more fruit – so too does a human being's body face the same cycle of birth, death, and rebirth to die again. Death comes through all living things on earth, naturally.

God did not send His only Son to show us the path to a physical existence. As Paul wrote, "As all die in Adam [**Man**], so all will be made alive in Christ." Therefore, Jesus was born of the same mortal death that all human beings are born of .. so the resurrection of his dead body shows the power of God.

We are called by God to Resurrect from our mortal being states, as Spiritual beings. We must die, in the sense that our natural love of the flesh ceases driving our brains. We must die of ego so our souls may be reborn with a love of God.

We are called by God to have the faith of Jesus, so that after our physical bodies are dead and buried we can Ascend to Heaven and stop paying for our sins by naturally recycling to sin again.

In the alternate Gospel reading from Luke, we are in attendance with the "women who had come with Jesus from Galilee." We walk with them to the tomb.

Just as those women symbolize sacrifice, in their commitment to follow Jesus, **we too must be subservient to Jesus**. The men who followed Jesus from Galilee had all run away and were in hiding, which symbolized a lack of subservience.

When those women servants arrived at the tomb to put spices on the corpse of a departed loved one, they encountered "two men in dazzling clothes" – angels of the Lord. Their encounter was just like the one Cornelius experienced.

[**Aside**: Angels visit with those who are God-fearing, generous, and pray often.]

The first thing that was said by the angels to those women – which is also spoken to **us**, as if we were there with them – was:

"Why do you look for the living among the dead?"

Think about that for a minute.

<pause>

Why would anybody think Jesus Christ might be found in a plastic egg or a hollow piece of chocolate, shaped like a rabbit? Those things only represent the cycle of worldly being, which is death.

The "hunt" for Jesus is within, not in a backyard or in a cemetery. We need to seek Jesus through the Father.

When the angel who spoke to the women of Jesus said, "[The fleshy body of Jesus] is not here, but has risen," those same women had wept and mourned a death less than three weeks earlier. They cried then because their relative Lazarus had become ill, died and was buried in another tomb, in Bethany. Jesus then came and said, "Lazarus, come out!"

We are called to be Lazarus, as he was called to be a reborn Jesus, touched by Christ and resurrected from death. Lazarus, although already stinking of death, was saved from repeating that cycle - live to sin, die for sins.

[**Aside**: The stench of death is metaphor for sins committed for worldly gains. Baptism by water is metaphor for washing off that stench that all bodies of flesh, who are all born of death, carry with them wherever they go.]

Why would the women **not** be looking for their risen loved one elsewhere, if they truly served God, the Father of the Son of Man?

Since Jesus had raised Lazarus from death, why wouldn't the same Godly force raise the human Jesus too?

Do you look upon a cross of death, one hanging on a wall, and seek Jesus there? Do you imagine the tomb Jesus was buried in as typical of a humanly forever resting place? Do you see a memorial garden, a cemetery, or an urn filled with crematory ashes as idols of death that reflect the gateway to heaven?

Or, do you look into your heart to find the risen Lord and eternal life?

The angel then reminded the women then – as the angel reminds us today – "Remember how he told you that the Son of Man must be handed over to sinners, and be crucified, and on the third day rise again?"

Can you not see how we must find Jesus by becoming Jesus reborn?

It is us who are also handed over to sinners, because being born of death means a life full of sins to repent. It is us who also must be crucified, such that we need to have our egos nailed to the cross of Salvation, until they are dead. Then, after **three days** dead, we can be resurrected as Jesus Christ.

**Three** is not literal, in our cases, but figurative. Can you see how the number **three** is representative of the **Trinity**?

Our three days dead mean we must enter into three phases of searching:

1. We must become the Son;

2. We must sacrifice all of our self-will to the Father;

3. The Father will redeem the Son by the Holy Spirit.

We have to be dead of self-ego throughout that search.

The cross is the Trinity, where the vertical is the Son, the horizontal is the Father, and the point where they intersect is the union of the two, by the Holy Spirit.

That intersection does not represent the brain, but the heart. Therefore, the cross does more than tell us how Jesus died for our sins. The cross symbolizes our own death, so we can be resurrected as Jesus Christ. That resurrection is how Jesus dies to forgive us of our mortal sins. By his death he can be reborn in us.

Enjoy your pink, blue, and yellow *Peeps* when you get home. Hopefully the Easter Bunny left you a tasty surprise, like the joys commonly left behind by Santa Claus and the

# Easter Sermons: Easter Sunday, Year C

Tooth Fairy.

But, by all means, remember the words of David, who sang:

> "I shall not die, but live, and declare the works of the Lord. The Lord has punished me sorely, but he did not hand me over to death."

> "The same stone which the builders rejected has become the chief cornerstone."

Amen

# SECOND SUNDAY OF EASTER

# YEAR C

**Relevant readings:**
Acts 5:27-32
Psalm 118 or
Psalm 150
Revelation 1:4-8
John 20:19-31

## Blessed are the believers whose proof is within

I am sure you have heard the proverb, "Seeing is believing."

It means, "You need to see something before you can accept that it really exists or occurs."

In one regard, we are given sight as a way of leading us to find truths and answers. We read Scripture with our eyes and Scripture is how we do find answers and truths in that which is written.

Still, our eyes often play tricks on us. Con artists at carnivals have made lots of money from the bets of suckers who thought they were able to follow which cup hid the ball.

From that failure of eyesight comes the saying, "The hand is quicker than the eye."

Still, sometimes the eyes imagine things that are not exactly as reality proves those things to be. For instance, just recently a report came out that the *Elasmotherium sibiricum* lived in a refuge as little as 29,000 years ago.

The *Elasmotherium sibiricum* is a Siberian unicorn. We imagine a unicorn to look like a white horse with rainbow colored tails and manes (and pink hooves). Our daughters love to have posters of unicorns like that, as well as soft, fluffy dolls that look like horses with a magical horn.

The reality is a *Elasmotherium sibiricum* looked more like a woolly mammoth rhinoceros, with only one horn and no tusks.

Rashevsky, under supervision of A.F. Brant

Robert Tippett

The lessons of this week point to how we see Jesus Christ; and like our views of unicorns, there is blindness that we Christians must deal with, based on his fitting our mental imaginations and our desire for visual proof.

Obviously, when we read in John's Gospel, "Have you believed because you have seen me? Blessed are those who have not seen and yet have come to believe," the question is posed to us. While Jesus asked that question to Thomas, we are the same doubters in need of proof. We must make that connection - we are each Thomas - because we also fall into that 'seeing is believing' category.

That famous question and quote from Jesus was made to the disciple "Thomas (who was called the Twin)." The Greek word for "twin" (thus the nickname for Thomas) is "*didymus.*"

This Gospel remembrance is how the moniker "Doubting Thomas" came into being. While Thomas is identified as "one of the twelve," meaning he was a lead disciple of Jesus (the same as Judas was "one of the twelve"), Thomas is identified as a "Twin." That means he physically had a twin sibling; but it also means, symbolically, that Thomas had two sides of himself - the faithful follower and the doubtful believer.

Since **we** are representative of all of the disciples – individually and collectively – as the ones who claim to be Christian today, we also share this duality of Thomas.

We need to see ourselves as Thomas, and not as one of the other trembling followers of Jesus. The man who had just been crucified is said to have resurrected and is alive again. However, we were not there when that miracle occurred. Thomas is then our "twin" personality in absentia.

We are doubters when we say, "Before I submit fully to belief in Jesus as having been resurrected, I need real proof of that." No matter how much fun it is to say "I believe Jesus died and resurrected," there is that scientific element that offers the seed of doubt to grow.

This doubt is no different than telling our daughters we believe in unicorns, when our adult minds say, "I need to see skeletal remains of a unicorn … remains that I can touch, take samples from, and put under an electron microscope and do carbon dating on ... before I will really believe."

Those whose beliefs come from having actually put their finger on the nail holes in the hands of Jesus and stuck their whole hand into the spear wound on Jesus's side are told, "Do not doubt but believe." Belief comes from personal experience, not from hearsay.

We read the stories of some who have had personal experiences with the resurrected Jesus. Paul was one. Paul (as Saul) was likewise a doubter, but his life was changed from such a **real** encounter.

Still, Jesus said, "**Blessed** are those who have not seen and yet have come to believe."

We should hear the word "**Blessed**" and interpret that as having the defined meaning that states "Consecrated" or "Made Holy."

When you see that one word defined in its highest sense ... which comes from the voice of the resurrected Lord making "Blessed" qualify for the highest definition – Jesus said (in paraphrase), "Those who are filled with the Holy Spirit have come to believe in Christ Jesus because they were touched by him Spiritually."

This means Jesus said more than (again I paraphrase), "If you say you believe in me without having ever seen me physically, then God will bless you for being a disciple of Jesus." The use of "blessed" here is on a lower level of meaning, as the definition, "Given happiness, pleasure, and contentment."

This means we are **not** made holy or righteous by faith alone. Doubting Thomas and the other hiding-in-fear-disciples had only taken one step in the right direction because they had seen Jesus do some stuff ... none of which they fully understood.

They would understand once they received the Spirit and Peace was within them. Still, see with your heart-led mind how touching the wounds of Jesus made Thomas (and the others who so touched his wounds) **in** Jesus. The power of touch then became like Jesus said, "I am **in** the Father and the Father is **in** me." (John 14:11)

Jesus then also said, "You will realize that I am **in** my Father, and you are **in** me, and I am **in** you." (John 14:20) When Thomas touched the risen Lord for proof, he was **in** Jesus **AND** then Jesus was **in** Thomas.

Seeing was no longer believing, as being one with Jesus occurred. The meaning of "**Blessed** are those who have not seen and yet have come to believe" was the aspect of **being made holy** through personally **felt** experience.

In the reading from the Acts of the Apostles, we see how the temple police had rounded up the disciples and brought them before the council and the high priest.

They had all become replications of Jesus by then. The problem the ranking officials thought they had eliminated had then been multiplied by twelve (or more).

When the disciples trembled and hid behind locked doors, they had no **Peace** with them. The disciples of Jesus had not yet been **Blessed** and **made holy** by <u>receiving</u> the Spirit.

Prior to having their hearts opened by the **touch** of the resurrected Lord, they had no understanding that would lead any of them to say, "We must obey God rather than any human authority."

When they then added, "We are <u>witnesses</u> to these things, and so is the Holy Spirit whom God has given to those who obey him," the Apostles had **eyes** that no longer only worked on the physical level. Their beings were allowed **to see** spiritually, so their souls had been given the strength to face any human authority. As resurrections of Jesus, each apostle had received sight was from the highest authority.

That is how David sang, "The Lord is my strength and my song, and he has become my salvation." No one other than God provides both strength and redemption for eternity.

This is where John's writing in *The Revelation* commands

us to "Look!" This command speaks to us on a human level and on a spiritual level.

We are told **to see** and ordinary people (disciples) hear that order and begin searching their surroundings. Those who have been **Blessed** by the Holy Spirit search for God within.

That means to next be told, "He is coming with the clouds," makes one become a watcher of the skies, or one who knows the presence of Christ <u>within</u> is a misty presence that cannot be seen with the physical eyes. We must "Look!" through the Mind of Christ to see the Holy Spirit's presence.

This duality of disciple and Apostle, of believer in a God who is external and one whose faith is in God being within one's heart, is how everything that is written in the Holy Bible has surface meaning and deeper meaning. We need a higher mind helping us **see** the higher meaning that is intended to be found.

We see this in John writing "to the seven churches that are in Asia." Some think John wrote seven letters and dispatched those epistles to seven different places in first century Turkey.

Others see only one letter - *The Revelation of John* - which is the one epistle that was begrudgingly placed as the last book of the Holy Bible by the early Church council. As Canon, all Christianity has since become one with each of those seven churches. Every Christian reader of *The Revelation* can **see** how those seven churches refer only to the one Church of Christ [not a denomination, but a body of saints].

The number seven has higher, deeper meaning, more than simply representing a count of seven churches. The number seven represents **perfection**, simply because God rested on the seventh day of his perfect Creation.

Another way of saying God rested on the Sabbath is to say God brought **Peace** to the world then. The Sabbath was **Blessed** and **made Holy**. That was because on the Sabbath day God made his first priest, who would be seeded upon the earth – Adam. God made Adam of clay and breath, as earth being made one with heaven, formed in the Garden of Eden - heaven on earth.

Despite all the work the physical plane demands, time must be set aside so one can be at **Peace** with the Lord and reflect on his inner presence, so one is reminded of the union between the material and the spiritual.

That duality is how the number seven has both positive associations, while also having negative associations. Overall the number represent perfection; but perfection is impossible by Man alone. Perfection can only come through God.

Thus, when John wrote his letters to the seven churches, he pointed out the positive and the negative that each church was known to have created … so that all were known by God to be short of perfection … all were known to be short of showing they had fully received God's Holy Spirit within them.

During this Easter period, we need to see how important it is that we spend considerable time learning our faith, through knowing the tenets of our religion and all the Scriptures.

Just as John wrote in his Gospel, "Now Jesus did many other signs in the presence of his disciples, which are not written in this book. But these are written so that you may come to believe that Jesus is the Messiah, the Son of God, and that through believing you may have life in his name." We must progress beyond being a follower of Jesus, to being a leader **as Jesus**. We need to understand how it is the Holy Bible is indeed **Holy**.

The Easter season is the equivalent of the time Moses led the Israelites to Mount Sinai (or Horeb), where they waited forty days for Moses to come down with the Covenant. Following the week after the Passover and the days taken to reach the mount, Moses went up the mountain. He said he would return, but the Israelites feared he had died from seeing God. Their fear caused them to revert to pagan worship.

The Easter season is when we become like Moses (beyond a priest, and beyond being simply a disciple) and go up the mountain that Jesus Christ represents, so we talk with God through him. After forty days of learning – seeing the many signs that can't all be written down – we are then prepared to receive the Holy Spirit.

Our preparation **requires** work. Six days we work, and then we spend the Sabbath in **Peace** with the Lord. That means the Easter season is seven weeks of work (6 days a week) and rest (one day a week). That is forty-nine days total.

# Easter Sermons: Second Sunday of Easter, Year C

Following that training, we will reach the Day of Pentecost - the Fiftieth Day. Then, it will be time to pay attention "to him who loves us and freed us from our sins by his blood, and made us to be a kingdom, priests serving his God and Father."

We have been called to be high priests to the One God, through Jesus Christ.

That requires more than profession of belief. It requires the **acts** that make one become an Apostle.

We need to seek inner Peace ... the Peace of the Lord. We need to receive the Holy Spirit and become truly Blessed.

We need to be filled with an understanding that John saying, "Look! He is coming with the clouds," and understand how that means Jesus has already come as promised, **many times before**; and he is still coming within those who open their hearts to God.

*The Revelation of John* is a letter to us to seek the perfection God offers through the Holy Spirit. Without that power within us, guiding our actions of faith, giving us the strength to display that perfection - as sinners who have forever ceased sinning - then when we read "Jesus is coming with a cloud," we can only **see** through eyes that can only focus on the negative of our imperfection.

That side of our dual nature trembles when we read, "every eye will see him, even those who pierced him; and the tribes of the earth will wail." We must rise about that imperfection and seek the perfection of God.

Robert Tippett

If you watch the news today, it is easy to see how much that wailing has begun. This is because there is now a shortage of high priests who are deeply devoted to serving God, through Christ.

To have "a life in his name," we must "receive the Spirit" and have "Peace be with us" as a reborn Jesus, led by God in one's heart. Then, we can stand before any authority the world has to offer and tell them, "The God of our ancestors raised up Jesus, whom you had killed."

We can put the fear of God in them by saying, "We are witnesses to these things, and so is the Holy Spirit whom God has given to those who obey him."

"Blessed is he who comes in the name of the Lord." Blessed is he (or she) who comes as a reborn Jesus!

Amen

# Easter Sermons: Second Sunday of Easter, Year C

# THIRD SUNDAY OF EASTER

# YEAR C

**Relevant readings:**
Acts 9:1-6-20
Psalm 30
Revelation 5:11-14
John 21:1-19

## Which Easter Apostle are you more like?

This is the third Sunday of Easter. There is symbolism that should be seen in that statement.

The Easter season is when we are taught by the Lord to go beyond the state of discipleship and evolve into an Apostle.

# Easter Sermons: Third Sunday of Easter, Year C

This is Saint Andrew, but all Apostles have the halo of the Holy Spirit surrounding them.

Saint Andrew the Apostle by Yoan from Gabrovo, 19th century
Plamen Agov • studiolemontree.com

For Christians, Sunday is our Sabbath, such that it represents when we find peace and calm, as a day of rest so we can reconnect to the Lord.

The number three represents the Trinity, but on a level where there is a sense of **initial completion**, such that we begin to see three, but still need to learn how three becomes one.

Last week, as at other times before, I talked about the dualistic nature of life. We see that reflected in many of the stories in the Holy Bible, where two main characters meet: Abraham and Lot, Samson and Delilah, Moses and the Pharaoh, David and Goliath, Jesus and John the Baptist, Jesus and Nicodemus, and Jesus and the woman at the well … just to name a few.

Robert Tippett

In today's readings, in line with the Easter season being when **we** are called to serve the Lord completely, we find two Apostles of different histories, who are not together in one story. Today we see Paul (when he was known as Saul) and Peter (the most prominent of Jesus's disciples).

This dichotomy can be seen by our eyes as how **we** progress as Christians. Are **we** following a path more like Saul-Paul, or are **we** on a road more similar to Peter's?

Sts. Peter and Paul

There is more than what immediately meets the eye in these readings. It is easy to read how, "Saul, still breathing threats and murder against the disciples of the Lord, went to the high priest and asked him for letters to the synagogues of Damascus, so that if he found any who belonged to the Way, men or women, he might bring them bound to Jerusalem," was more like an atheist is today, or even a Islamic terrorist … and see nothing about ourselves in that character.

It is equally easy to read how, "When Simon Peter heard

that it was the Lord, he put on clothes, because he was naked, and jumped into the sea," and see how Peter was the first disciple, above all the rest, who fervently wanted to be close to Jesus. We can easily identify with that character.

Still, there are cracks in the appearance of both characters, cracks that are worthy of closer inspection.

In the reading from Acts, we see how Saul "fell to the ground and heard a voice," after "a light from heaven flashed around him" (and those with whom he travelled to Damascus).

Falling to the ground represents assuming a position of subservience ... as does bowing down and kneeling before one of importance. Because Saul **heard a voice** from heaven, we should be able to intuit that his soul was connected strongly to God. This means Saul was a devout believer of God ... but his way of serving God needed some serious adjusting.

As horrid as Saul's acts had been, he was known for his acts ... not his inaction. We see that when the Lord went to his servant Ananias and asked him to go see Saul. We read how Ananias said, "Lord, I have heard about this man, how much evil he has done to your saints in Jerusalem."

People don't spread rumours and talk about people who do nothing. Saul was a **doer**.

Now, in the reading from the Gospel of John, which I believe is a dream rather than an actual event, we can see that Peter was a doer too. We read that "Simon Peter said to the other disciples, "I am going fishing." Six of those then said, "We will go with you."

Think about that for a moment.

<pause>

According to one website I found:

> "**Gone fishing**" is an English idiom that is used in reference to someone who is completely unaware of all that is going on in his or her immediate surroundings. The person described in this manner has checked out from reality and may be daydreaming or just simply ignorant of the people and things in the vicinity." (www.wisegeek.org)

The site also adds:

> "In its most literal sense, this phrase refers to someone who has consciously removed himself from a situation. When the stress of modern life becomes a bit too much, an idyllic retreat can be just what is needed to regain a sense of calm. As a result, some people may take some time away from their routines to find a brief bit of relaxation, and this expression represents those getaways."

When this is realized, it becomes clearer to see how Peter was leading a majority of Jesus's disciples on something of a "working vacation," where the "work" was fishing.

Again, when you see this as being part of a dream, then the fishing element takes on the symbolic meaning of the time that Jesus told James and John of Zebedee, "I will make you fishers of men." This means the work is that of want-to-be Apostles, more than laziness ... but they were trying to catch fish, not men.

Of course, the main focus that John placed on Simon Peter was when Jesus (appearing as an old man) asked him three times, "Do you love me?" The answer given by Peter (twice) was, "Yes, Lord; you know that I love you."

While that may sound like Peter did love Jesus, the use of "*philō*" means "affectionate friendship" or "heartfelt consideration," and that realization somewhat weakens that feeling of "love." This is pronounced when one realizes that Jesus asked by using the word "*agapas*."

The word "*agapas*" means the kind of "love" that is more "to wish well to, to take pleasure in, to long for," and in particular, "to esteem" or "to have a reasoned love." This understanding shows that Jesus was asking if Peter wanted to have the Mind of Christ, to go along with the love of God that was already deeply seated in Peter's heart. Jesus was asking Peter if he had the esteem of Jesus that others had for Jesus.

Now, when Peter followed his affirmative answer by saying, "You know that I love you," and when he answered the third time, adding "Lord, you know everything," before he answered again, saying "You know that I love you." It can sound like Peter was answering much as Ezekiel did, when God asked him, "Mortal, can these dried bones live?"

While we read both Ezekiel and Peter say, "Lord, you know," the same meaning and intent is not the case.

Ezekiel's answer, "**You know**," was a statement about the all-knowing mind of God. However, the Greek word used by Peter was "*oidas*," which is rooted in "*eídō (oida)*," and literally means "to see."

Peter was not expressing faith that Jesus knew any more than he could observe. As such, Peter stated that his actions spoke for his love, as, "Lord, **you see** I love you."

This then leads one to recall the Passover Seder meal, when Jesus proved **he knew** Peter's heart, telling Peter he would betray Jesus three times before the cock crowed. Jesus could **see** Peter, whose actions showed his lack of true commitment to the ministry of Jesus: arguing about his feet being washed, cutting off a soldier's ear in anger, and losing faith when he tried to walk on water, just to name a few examples.

Along this line of thought, when "Simon Peter heard it was the Lord," we are told, "he put on some clothes, for he was naked."

"Naked" is how God "sees" us all; such that when Adam and Eve first realized they were uncovered, as God called out for them, they covered themselves with leaves. They did so because they thought they could keep God from knowing they had sinned.

The same pretence should be seen in the action of Peter to clothe himself, prior to presenting himself to the Lord. His first reaction was to cover himself - a sign of having something to hide.

As a contrast between Peter and Saul, we should see how

Easter Sermons: Third Sunday of Easter, Year C

Peter (and the other disciples) were invited to "Come and have some breakfast." Now, the word translated as "breakfast" is "*aristēsate*," which means to "dine" on a meal prior to the evening supper. It could be lunch or breakfast. However, the word "breakfast" is interesting as it literally means to "break **fast**," by eating after roughly 12 hours since one's last meal.

By Peter having been fed bread and fish – the same as the foods that fed the multitudes of 5,000 and 4,000 – he and the other disciples had been fed spiritual food. As John then stated that this was the third time Jesus had "appeared to the disciples after he was raised from the dead," there was a state of initial completion (symbolism of **three**) as to how to feed others.

This feeding then led to Jesus telling Peter, "Feed my lambs" and "Feed my sheep."

You do not literally go feed livestock in order to serve God, through Jesus Christ. You feed a flock with spiritual food ... knowledge that uplifts their souls.

Saul, on the other hand, had never been fed anything by Jesus. Instead, he was stricken with blindness and told to go to Damascus and await instructions. We are then told that Saul "for **three** days was without sight and neither ate nor drank."

In other words, Saul began a **fast**. After the Apostle Ananias touched Saul and filled him with the Holy Spirit – the **true** spiritual food – his blindness disappeared and he began to praise Jesus as the Messiah. His strength was regained by physical food, but he was baptized with Holy

Robert Tippett

Spirit, not water.

The link between Saul and Peter is Ananias, who represents an Apostle of Jesus Christ, one who has been touched by God and Christ. Saul would change his name to Paul. Simon Peter would be known as Saint Peter. Both would serve God through Christ, as each would be reborn as a new Jesus.

The point of this comparison-contrast today ... during this **third** Sunday of the Easter season ... is for you to ask yourself, "Which one of these two **disciples** do I model more?"

Are you one who is so fervent about your faith that you leave a wake of destruction along you path, so that people tremble when they see you coming?

Or, are you one who takes the happy-go-lucky, lazy day, "gone fishing" way of putting your religion in your back pocket, only to leave your faith on the shore as you drift naked and aimless on the waters of human existence?

When Ananias **heard** the voice of the Lord come to him in an auditory vision, he could not **see** the Lord with his physical eyes. Still, Ananias **knew** who called his name.

Do **you** have the ability to hear your name being called?

Do you need someone to tell you, "It is the Lord" who is standing before you ... "Listen to him!"?

Can you respond by answering, "Here I am, Lord"?

Or, do you require God send lightning bolts crashing all

around you, causing you to fall to the ground, so you are finally blinded ... no longer distracted by all the shiny objects this world has to offer?

Do you need something like that to happen so you will then be willing to follow the instructions of the Lord – **to serve Him**?

Or, do you make a show of your admiration for Jesus by wearing crucifix necklaces, putting fish emblems on your car, or leading Bible Study groups, so others can **see** your love ... all while you are hiding a trembling heart that is without God?

Does your true faith make you always capable of denying you are a Christian, if you ever feel threatened by the eyes of the world?

Only you can decide who you serve. Only you can determine what you believe and in whom or in what you have faith.

We are all like the fish in the sea ... like the one hundred fifty-**three** large fish pulled ashore by the disciples, in the unbroken net. We have all grown fat from living in this earthly world a long, long time. Thus we all have scales, like the ones that fell from Saul's eyes when he gained an ability to see the truth for the first time.

In John's other dream, found in the reading from *The Revelation*, we are included in that number, written as "a hundred fifty **three**" ("*hekaton pentēkonta **triōn***"). That number represents the final completion of a spiritual quest.

Numerologically 153 is reduced to $1 + 5 + 3 = 9$. Still, the Greek words state it like this: $100 + 50 + 3$, where each number has importance alone. One hundred is $10 \times 10$, or $1 + 0 + 0 = 1$. A one equates to an individual, but "a hundred" is a divine elevation of one. Fifty can then be seen as a statement about the counting of the omer, or Pentecost - the Fiftieth day. One will be elevated divinely on that numbered day. Finally, three is the Trinity, where Father + Son + Holy Spirit are One.

In multiplication, 9 is the product of $3 \times 3$. The number 153, when seen as a nine, reflects the end of one journey. It symbolizes completion. Three represent an initial completion of a journey. Nine symbolizes fulfillment of a goal. The number of fish caught are then a statement about the end of those fishermen's work. As a three they mastered fishing for fish. As a nine they would master fishing for men's souls.

Jesus, in unrecognizable form, told them where to cast their net. Their net was the Holy Spirit of God, which cannot be broken. Once in that net, there is no return to the depth of the waters from which a soul comes.

Therefore, we each are one of "**every** creature in heaven and on earth and under the earth and in the sea," such that we are called upon to **sing** praises.

**SING!**

> "To the one seated on the throne and to the Lamb be blessing and honor and glory and might forever and ever!"

Easter Sermons: Third Sunday of Easter, Year C

**SING!**

> "You have turned my wailing into dancing; you have put off my sack-cloth and clothed me with joy. Therefore my heart sings to you without ceasing; Oh Lord my God, I will give you thanks for ever."

Amen

# FOURTH SUNDAY OF EASTER

# YEAR C

**Relevant readings:**
Acts 9:36-43
Psalm 23
Revelation 7:9-17
John 10:22-30

## The grass is always greener where the Good Shepherd tends his flock

In the past, I have written about the Aesop fable called "The Shepherd Boy and the Wolf." It is more commonly known as, "The Boy Who Cried Wolf."

I feel the need to repeat what I have written about the misinterpretation of that fable, which is said to be: "Liars are not believed even when they speak the truth."

While that conclusion sounds logical, it is wrong.

In reality, liars are often believed, as they know how to take advantage of the trust people naturally award to others. Thus, liars become bad shepherds who are only **not** trusted after their lies have come to light. The "moral of this story" has nothing to do with lying.

Without reading it aloud, I refer you to the handout on the bus stop bench that retells the fable (according to PROJECT GUTENBERG EBOOK AESOP'S FABLES):

> *"There was once a young Shepherd Boy who tended his sheep at the foot of a mountain near a dark forest. It was rather lonely for him all day, so he thought upon a plan by which he could get a little company and some excitement.*
>
> *He rushed down towards the village calling out "Wolf, Wolf," and the villagers came out to meet him, and some of them stopped with him for a considerable time. This pleased the boy so much that a few days afterwards he tried the same trick, and again the villagers came to his help.*
>
> *But shortly after this a Wolf actually did come out from the forest, and began to worry the sheep, and the boy of course cried out "Wolf, Wolf," still louder than before. But this time the villagers, who had been fooled twice before, thought the boy was again deceiving them, and nobody stirred to come to his help.*

*So the Wolf made a good meal off the boy's flock, and when the boy complained, the wise man of the village said:*

*"A liar will not be believed, even when he speaks the truth."*

Some sources present a milder version of this story that was actually written by Aesop. The milder version embellishes the story with extra details, which veer one away from the eventual conclusion that warns against lying. Either way, the basic story draws an questionable moral.

From basic memory of this story we have all heard before, I want you to realize that the shepherd is always a boy ... not a man. Shepherding is a child's responsibility. Grown-ups have better things to do than sit and daydream, while sheep graze in a field.

You will recall that David was just a boy when God called Samuel to anoint a son of Jesse. David, the youngest, was not there with his six brothers who were to be viewed by Samuel, because he was too young and he had been sent out to tend to Jesse's sheep.

Also, on the night Jesus was born in Bethlehem, an angel appeared to shepherds out in the fields. Since a shepherd had (and still has) a subordinate position in the societal hierarchy of times past, fathers sent their sons (even daughters) to do the work of tending flocks. While youthfulness is required, shepherds were usually boys not yet grown to full adulthood.

Still, when we see capitalized words say "Good Shepherd," our mind automatically sees an adult. We see pictures of a bearded Jesus holding a stray lamb in his arms. Jesus is the Good Shepherd, even though a regular shepherd is just a boy.

Now, rather than a projection of how the shepherd boy in Aesop's fable was a "bad shepherd," it is worthwhile to see him in the light of being just a child. From that perspective, it is not accurate to portrayal the boy as a liar, simply because he cried out "Wolf!"

When the wolf did appear, the boy **honestly** screamed out for help. In my interpretation of Aesop's fable, the worst assumption that can be projected on the boy shepherd is that he was bored and in need of mature guidance. When all the important elements are then seen in place: shepherd, sheep, the master's flock, the villagers, and the threat of a wolf, then the aspect of mature guidance changes the narrative significantly.

It is then important to view this fable in a new light. See how the shepherd boy reflects Jesus Christ, so the master's sheep become the souls of the villagers who leave their souls in the care of Christ while they go about their normal lives. This means "the Master's sheep" are all Christians.

Jesus is the Son of God, in the same manner that David was the son of Jesse. God sent his Son out to watch over His flock, just as Jesse saw his boy, David, as the only one left to send and handle that responsibility. Jesse did not see David as King of the Israelite material, not at his young age, so David was not presented to Samuel. Instead, Jesse sent David to watch over his sheep. Similarly, Jesus told

Pilate he was not a king (indirectly), saying his kingdom was not of the earthly realm. God did not see His Son as King of the Jews material. Both sons had greater roles destined for them to play.

The wolf is then sin, which is an agent of Satan, who loves stealing souls and killing their chances of returning to heaven. In this way, wolves in sheep's clothing form their own flocks, misleading sheep to follow their voices, being bad shepherds. Children are not fully capable of being bad shepherds, as that role is left for adults who were not taught the proper path to adulthood as children. Still, a son would be more responsible than would a "hired hand." A son of a father would cry out a danger was present (even if there was none visible), whereas a hired hand (as an adult) would run away in fear that danger existed, when danger showed its true face.

Because the cry "Wolf!" came from the mouth of a babe, the innocence here says no lies were the intent. If one wants to call a test or drill a lie, one has drawn the wrong conclusion. If calling out "Wolf!" in order to test the system is lying, then fire alarm drills and Civil Defense sirens being tested is lying to the public.

Testing is necessary and we adults understand this. When people stop responding to tests, when the real threat happens no one responds. Then, you find out how important it is to always respond to a warning call, because test practice makes one vigilant and safe.

In the Gospel reading today we hear Jesus responding to a question posed by a group identified by John as "the Jews."

# Easter Sermons: Fourth Sunday of Easter, Year C

They asked, "How long will you keep us in suspense? If you are the Messiah, tell us plainly."

Jesus replied, "I have told you, and you do not believe. The works that I do in my Father's name testify to me; but you do not believe, because you do not belong to my sheep. My sheep hear my voice. I know them, and they follow me. I give them eternal life, and they will never perish. No one will snatch them out of my hand. What my Father has given me is greater than all else, and no one can snatch it out of the Father's hand. The Father and I are one."

Having heard me draw a comparison to Aesop's Shepherd Boy; think about this exchange now with a fresh set of eyes.

Can you hear "the Jews" as "the villagers" and Jesus as "the shepherd boy"?

<pause>

Can you hear the Jews asking Jesus, "How long will you keep crying out "Wolf!" to test us? If you are the Messiah, tell us plainly, so we will know if we should ignore your calls or keep dropping everything to come to your aid."

Can you hear the words of Jesus being, "I have told you the wolf is always near, and you do not believe. The calls I make I do in my Master's name. Those calls testify to me as a Good Shepherd of His sheep; but you do not believe and heed the call, because you do not belong to my sheep. The **souls** of my sheep hear my voice. I know them, and they follow me, as my Holy Mind guides them. I give them eternal life through preparedness, and they will never perish. They always respond, so they are safe from Satan and no one will snatch them out of my hand. Through the Holy Spirit, the Master has given me a responsibility that is greater than anything a bad shepherd can offer, and no one can snatch the Holy Spirit out of the Master's hand. The Master and I are one because of the Holy Spirit."

In this story from John's Gospel, the Jews become so angered that they attempt to stone Jesus to death. They reasoned, Jesus was "a mere man, claiming to be God." They saw his calls as heresy.

In Aesop's fable, the anger of the villagers caused their indifference to respond to a real danger call, which allowed the wolf to treat himself to a great many of the Master's sheep. Full of ruined souls, the wolf then snuck away into the **darkness** of the forest.

The Good Shepherd escaped unharmed … in both cases. Jesus took his disciples to the other side of the Jordan for the winter; and the shepherd boy of Aesop's mind was left alive, but with a smaller flock to tend.

In the vision John had, which is written in *The Revelation*, we hear all the souls that have been saved by the call of the Lamb of God singing out:

> "For **the Lamb** at the center of the throne **will be their shepherd**, and he will guide them to springs of the water of life."

Jesus Christ is the Lamb of God **AND** he is the Good Shepherd whose voice the souls of his sheep hear and heed. The "water of life" is the Holy Spirit that connects to each of the Master's souls.

As such, the souls of the saved have ignored their "villager" selves and all become led by the voice of the Good Shepherd within. The villagers are no longer just "the Jews" that ruled the Temple of Jerusalem, but all who lord over churches and synagogues today. The souls of all Christians and Jews who are the sheep of Jesus Christ are those led beside the still waters that restore them to true faith.

Each adds to what John saw:

> "Before me was a great multitude that no one could count, from every nation, from all tribes and peoples and languages, standing before the throne and before the Lamb, robed in white, with palm branches in their hands."

John saw many souls resurrected to eternal life, filled with the water of life. They had all ceased chasing after the busy work of the village, and become the children of God. Jesus had become the Good Shepherd of lost souls, who rejoiced in having been found and saved.

The boy shepherd had rescued each sheep, so each sheep was led by the Mind of the Good Shepherd. Each sheep knew the danger of not having that love of God within and the voice of Christ guiding them. They are who called out to those still lost ... still left behind ... crying out, "Wolf!"

The danger is real, even if Satan cannot be seen. He lurks in the darkness ... hidden in the forest ... watching ... waiting ... plotting. He is away from the light of the Lord. Satan sneaks into sheepfolds by night, like a thief; and he dresses up like sheep, in order to be accepted as a leader (as the false shepherd).

The boy shepherd is then like an Apostle of the Father, as a sheep of the Master, led by the Mind of the Good Shepherd. This is like we heard Jesus instruct Peter last week, when he told him, "Feed my lambs," "Tend my sheep," and "Feed my sheep." The <u>sheep of the Master</u> are child shepherds, all speaking from the Mind of Jesus Christ.

They **ARE** Jesus reborn … but they have the innocence of children. No egos or self-aggrandizing of one's mental capacities can make one holy enough to be **THE GOOD SHEPHERD**. Only Jesus is that. Only the lowliest of egos will allow Jesus to take control over their actions.

We are mere men (and women) … not allowed to claim to be God. Therefore, "the Jews" were right to know "mere men" cannot possibly be God.

However, their souls were not sheep of the Lord, so they could not hear the voice of Christ in Jesus of Nazareth.

<pause>

The other day, my wife said how it would seem that Jesus would identify as a Socialist, because he went after one lost lamb, leaving the rest behind. She said that disregard of the majority, for the good of the minority, was an element of Socialism.

I told her that no "–ism" can hold a candle to Jesus Christ and true Christianity.

# Easter Sermons: Fourth Sunday of Easter, Year C

A Socialist is one of philosophical thought, not the Mind of Christ. A Socialist attacks the majority, in order to serve the minority will. A Socialist is a wolf of Satan who threatens all flocks, most of which cannot hear the voice of Jesus Christ.

Listen to how Jesus told the Jews, "You do not believe, because you do not belong to my sheep. My sheep hear my voice. I know them, and they follow me."

Socialists have no religion leading them, thus they reject the notion of being Christians. Socialists do not believe in Jesus Christ. Therefore, they do not belong to the flock tended and fed by the Good Shepherd.

Socialists do not hear the voice of the Lamb or the voice of God, so they do not follow the guidance of the Mind of Christ. Christianity is not their core platform to do **GOOD**.

Because they refuse to answer the call, "Wolf!" Jesus is not their name, and they do not act as would Jesus.

The world can be saved by Christianity; but as the souls who were before the throne and the Lamb "cried out in a loud voice, "Salvation belongs to our God who is seated on the throne, and to the Lamb!"" no "-ism" can ever save a soul.

Christianity is a lifestyle that philosophers attempt to explain ... poorly.

People do not save the world through devised plans and written rules, such as, "It is hereby written that a boy will guard all the souls of a village, until which time a wolf is sighted. Then, said boy will cry out loudly, so that the villagers shall run to save the sheep and the boy."

It may be written as law, but where the heart leads the mind will follow. No one has his or her heart and soul in the written law ... especially not lawyers ...because one cannot hear the voice of the Good Shepherd leading that law.

Adult people are like children grown up, easily bored. When bored, people begin making up new rules and new games to play.

Still, Apostles cannot save the world either. They simply make themselves available, so others can see there is a different path to be followed. The world can only be saved by God; but the world must actually take steps towards that end.

Apostles demonstrate how to take those steps, but each soul must stand and walk alone (inspired by God, as the self's Good Shepherd).

In the reading from Acts we hear of "a disciple whose name was Tabitha." She "was devoted to good works and acts of charity." Tabitha "became ill and died."

Likewise, there are people in our society that do good works and serve charitably so others can find some solace to life's pains. Unfortunately, all acts and deeds of mortals are as temporary as the people who do them.

Because Tabitha died, the people whose lives Tabitha had affected mourned her death. This sorrow led for some to call for the Apostle Peter to come, as they knew Peter was a reborn miracle worker. Peter was like Jesus.

Peter came; but it was not he that raised Tabitha back to life.

Peter removed all the distractions from around him and he knelt down, praying to God for guidance. Peter was led by the Mind of Christ to say, "Tabitha, get up."

And Peter was aided by God above, who returned life to a good woman whose name means, "Beauty."

God sent Beauty back into the lives of others, so that others could be saved through her. Tabitha was resurrected by God, so Tabitha could become a female Jesus, led by the Mind of the Good Shepherd.

By the time John had his vision written in *The Revelation*; Peter and Tabitha had become two of that great multitude who John saw praising God and Christ in heaven.

Heaven is a place where only holy souls can gather. Holy souls used to belong to sheep that could hear the voice of the Good Shepherd and whose lives were washed clean of sins because they heeded the warning call, "Wolf!"

During this Easter season, the lessons are designed to show us the call to be added to the flock of the Good Shepherd. We are supposed to learn the value of good works and acts of charity. We are supposed to learn to listen for the call of our Lord.

As souls are grazing in the field, away from our normal lives. Our bodies busily attend to personal wants and desires in the "village" of a worldly existence; but we each need to be alert, able to hear when our name is called.

Our name might be called when we have strayed too far from the flock and are close to being lost. Our name might be called when the sins of Satan are lurking, waiting for us to wander into his grasp.

Easter is when we learn to hear and shout out, "Here I am, Lord. Save me! Tell me what to do!"

Easter season is a time to become dedicated to the Lord, where we consecrate our **selves** as temples of God. We do that as devoted disciples ... willing to learn. We do that through prayer, seeking guidance and repentance. We do that by good works and acts of charity that benefit others.

The life of a true Christian always comes with tests. We must be willing to take all tests, no matter how needless our childish minds see them to be, in hindsight.

We must see the truth of Christ, even when others claim our religion is lies. We must learn to pass the tests God sends us, so we too can be clothed in white robes that have been washed clean in the blood of the Lamb.

To reach that point, we must feel assured:

> "Though I walk through the valley of the shadow of death, I shall fear no evil; for you are with me; your rod and your staff, they comfort me."

Amen

# Easter Sermons: Fourth Sunday of Easter, Year C

# FIFTH SUNDAY OF EASTER

# YEAR C

**Relevant readings:**
Acts 11:1-18
Psalm 148
Revelation 21:1-6
John 13:31-35

## You are what you eat, so choose your foods carefully

I remember watching part of a television show quite a while back, where some show host had a Jewish rabbi as a guest. The rabbi was explaining what Jews were allowed to eat and why certain animals or parts of animals were forbidden.

# Easter Sermons: Fifth Sunday of Easter, Year C

I seem to recall there was some confusion about whether turkey was kosher or not.

I also watched some other show on the Food Channel, where this guy would go around the world eating some of the most disgusting things known to man, which to the locals was standard fare (somewhat).

In one episode he went to Cambodia. There, he went to an open-air food market where one vendor actually sold cockroaches as food.

A Cambodian gentleman that accompanied the food taster as he shopped recalled his memories of eating those insects as a child. He said they ate cockroaches because his family was very poor, living in the jungle. When hard times yielded scarce food, they would eat insects. When they found a swarm of cockroaches, they would sizzle them in a wok and serve them with rice. However, the man stressed that he hated having to eat cockroaches; and he pointed out how cockroaches was a source of food **only** to those who could not afford to purchase better foods. Such impure food was forced upon natives by starvation.

I also recall watching another program long ago that explored the disparities of the different castes of India. One segment documented the life of an Untouchable, which meant his family had been delegated to the lowest Caste in India. The man had lepers as parents, but he displayed no signs of any bodily deformity. Still, he could not mix with those of higher castes.

He had married another Untouchable and had children

with his wife. To feed his family, he became known as a rat catcher. Rats damaged the crops of those Indians who had land, so the rat catcher did a service to those farmers by catching the rats. The man got to keep the rats as a food stuff, which he would feed to his family. Obviously, in India only Untouchables would eat rats.

In America, if you go to Louisiana you learn that swamp rats are a delicacy. Many restaurants serve nutria - "a river rat" the size of a beaver - along with other foods that are forbidden from Jewish mouths: crayfish, shrimp, crab, oysters, and [of course] alligator.

Jews are forbidden from eating seafood that does not have fins and scales, which includes catfish (although young catfish have the appearance of scales). *Boudin* and *Andouille* - pork sausages - are another reason for Jews to avoid Louisiana.

You might know that barbecue ribs and flanks were once only eaten by poor people, those who took the leftovers – unwanted cuts of meat – and found ways to make them good to the taste. Pit cooked pork has long been a staple in the deep south of North America and in Hawaii. Still, Jews are forbidden from eating pork, because it has a split hoof and does not chew its cud.

Personally, I have a fairly simple diet. Almost everything I have found served to me at dinner time, I have eaten some of it, if not all. I like barbecue and regularly eat it. I have never eaten a rat of any kind, and do not find nutria appealing enough to try. I do not like the taste of crayfish, nor the messiness of eating it, so it is not a personal choice.

# Easter Sermons: Fifth Sunday of Easter, Year C

In my history, I learned at the age of two that I am never to eat pickled beets. I tried them once, and they crossed my lips only twice – going in and coming out. I will never eat pickled beets again; and I can assure you that cockroaches and rats have been added to my own "forbidden list" of foods.

In the reading from Acts today, Peter had to explain to his fellow "apostles and believers who were in Judea" that he had dined with Gentiles. Not only were Jews forbidden from eating certain meats, they were forbidden from even associating with non-Jews.

Part of that reasoning is non-Jews might be used to eating pork, cockroaches, rats, and even pickled beets to excess; but that did not make it okay for Jews to eat the same foods. Because there is a saying, "The way to a man's heart is through his stomach," there is danger in dining with those whose heart is not a home for YAHWEH.

<u>Temptation</u> is why a Jew must stay clear of Gentiles and their foods. If you dine with them and find a taste for what they eat, then you might acquire a taste for the most forbidden food … food for thought.

Remember the fruit from the tree of knowledge of good and evil? Just because Adam and Eve ate that once, does not mean that God said it was okay to be eaten forever afterwards.

Now the Gospel reading today is short and sweet and to the point. Jesus told his disciples – those who would become "apostles and believers" after his death – "I give you a **new** commandment, that <u>you love one another</u>."

Robert Tippett

It is important to realize that Jesus saved that one **new** tidbit of advice for **after** "Judas had gone out" of the upper room. Judas left to betray Jesus and set off the glorification process. Had Judas still been at the Seder meal when Jesus gave that **new commandment**, and had Judas not hung himself afterwards, then the other disciples – who would become "apostles and believers" after Jesus's death – would have been forced to forgive Judas and dine with him, like nothing bad had happened.

They would have to love Judas as much as the other disciples, had the story played out that way.

That would have been like forcing someone who hates pickled beets to eat pickled beets. It would be like being forced to eat of the fruit of the knowledge of good and evil, even though you had been told not to, by God Himself.

Jesus knew Judas was led by evil in his heart, so Jesus waited until Judas Iscariot left to do his dirty deed, before adding that new commandment. That kept the good disciples from having to ever sit and dine with an evil influence, knowing of evil's presence, but pretending all was good.

If you put that in a modern perspective, to be forced to dine with Judas would be like knowing an Islamic terrorist has killed before and promised to kill again – not just random murder, but targeted murder of non-Muslims [i.e.: Christians and Jews] - but being told to offer him the Sacraments. It would be like forced to **love** having yourself and/or your family killed by hatred.

That would then be like Jesus telling future Christians to

invite terrorists to move into your neighborhood, so they can kill those whom you love. Thank God Judas left before His Son told his disciples to love one another, adding "As I have loved you, so you must love one another."

If you think that includes Judas, then you might as well think Jesus said to eat cockroaches and rats during the next Passover Seder meal, rather than matzo, charred lamb bones and bitter herbs.

He did not say that. Again, thank God.

It is important to remember that when Jesus said he knew he would be betrayed, he added: "Woe to that man who betrays the Son of Man! It would be better for him if he had not been born."

That means Jesus did not come to change and laws of Moses. Jesus did not instruct his disciples to love the whole wide world – unconditionally.

He just added one **new** commandment, which was for that band of brothers and their families – all of who were disciples of Jesus and believers of his holiness – to love each other as one family of Christ, while remaining Jewish and children of God.

To clarify this a little more, Jesus then added to that **new commandment**: "Just as I have loved you, you also should love one another. By this everyone will know that you are my disciples, if you have love for one another."

It was a command to love one another, like the Three Musketeers loved one another:

"All for one and one for all!" they swore as an oath.

ALL FOR ONE -- AND -- ONE FOR ALL         6.3.74

It means the disciples were to maintain all the other Jewish laws in place. That means meeting with Jews who did not know about Jesus, to tell them the Good News – The Messiah has come!

That was the meaning of "love thy neighbor." However, once that group started saying the name Jesus over and over, because a bond of love kept that group together through being known by that name, their love for one another would evolve them into Jewish Christians, separate from Jews.

By taking in new disciples and teaching them to love one another, as Jesus had done for them, the group would grow stronger as it grew larger. Thus, loving one another means supporting one another, like one loves family in that way ... the family of Christ.

Spreading the Gospel then becomes an act of loving your neighbor. Telling other Jews, who are not part of your family in Christ, invites other Jews to join in that **new** bond of love.

# Easter Sermons: Fifth Sunday of Easter, Year C

Loving you enemy means not going into the places where non-Jews live and expecting non-Jews to welcome you with open arms ... especially when a Jew will avoid contact with a non-Jew. You love your enemy by allowing them to eat pork, cockroaches, rats, or any of the other Jewish forbidden foods, without condemnation.

That means loving you enemy is shown by allowing your enemy to be you enemy, by not egging your enemy to further anger.

Now, when you understand Jesus's **new commandment** to his non-betraying disciples, and knowing Peter was one of those who heard that commandment, you can understand why Peter was "criticized" by his fellow "apostles and believers" ... who loved him as family.

You see, love of one another leads one to confront another who breaks a law ... an old commandment of the Lord. That is part of the love that bonds a Church together. It is mandatory maintenance.

That is why the New Testament is mostly made up of letters written, Epistles penned by Apostles, showing love for other apostles. It means loving one another by sending reminders about what laws must be followed, at all costs.

Therefore, it was love of his brothers in Christ that led Peter to explain his vision about being commanded to eat forbidden meats. It was love that had Peter tell his family how a heavenly voice was heard, saying "What God has made clean, you must not call profane."

That does not mean that all "four-footed animals of the

earth, wild beasts, reptiles and birds" are forevermore approved for eating. It says, "If you are lost in a strange land and starving, praying for food, then should God send you cockroaches or rats to meet your prayers of survival, consider **those** as clean, and no longer profane."

"Kill and eat!"

In that vein of cleanliness, it was love that had the Roman centurion, Cornelius, send men to get Simon called Peter and escort him to Caesarea. Because Cornelius was "a God-fearing man, who gave generously to those in need and prayed to God regularly," an angel of God was sent to Cornelius, telling him to send for Peter.

It was love for one another that led Cornelius to have his relatives and **close friends** be at his house to greet Peter when he arrived with his **close friends** in ministry. It was love for one another that had Cornelius fall down before Peter, honoring Peter's presence in his house.

It was love of one another that God had pious Gentiles meet with pious Christian Jews, so **all** of the Romans in Cornelius's house could be witnessed by Christian Jews as Gentiles who spoke in the tongues of the Holy Spirit. Love had Peter and friends stay with Cornelius – a forbidden Gentile – for a few more days.

It was a love for one another that Peter asked his fellow "apostles and believers in Judea," "Who was I that I could hinder God?"

It is so very important in this Easter season, when we are called to **learn** all the meaning of the teachings of Jesus

Christ. To open oneself up to a higher knowledge that we must receive, we must see ourselves as "little children," **thirsting** for the knowledge of God's Christ.

We become the little children of Jesus Christ when we love one another, as Jesus Christ has shown he loves us. As the little children of Jesus's family, everyone should know that we are Christians because we love all Christians, and all Christians love us.

For those who have been glorified by the gifts of God's Holy Spirit, you are called to **teach** those little children who are in need of learning, just as Jesus showed his love by doing that for his disciples.

This is what God commanded his little children of Israel to do:

> "Fix these words of mine in your hearts and minds; tie them as symbols on your hands and bind them on your foreheads. Teach them to your children, talking about them when you sit at home and when you walk along the road, when you lie down and when you get up." (Deuteronomy 11:18-19)

We who call ourselves Christian, we who are of Gentile origin as non-Jews, we are called to understand the importance of not defiling our bodies and minds by showing a **special love**, one that is designated only for Christians, but can extend to anybody and everybody.

We should show non-Christians neighborly love, if they are our neighbors; but we should also allow non-Christians the space they need to not feel pressured by Christians.

Likewise, we should expect our non-Christian neighbors to give us the space we need, as Christians, to love one another. In that way we do unto others as we would have them do unto us.

We show love of one another by preferring to associate with others who believe in Jesus Christ and who are apostles through the Holy Spirit. That preference strengthens our abilities to "free associate" with the whole wide world.

Without the strength of the Holy Spirit being maintained by that love of Jesus Christ, we leave ourselves open to evil feeling weakness; and that becomes an invitation to destroy our family that is bonded by God's love. Love of one another keeps us strong in Christ.

The temptation is to save the world without first being taught how to save our own souls.

In John's vision told in *The Revelation*, we find that he saw a time when the old heaven and the old earth will have **passed away**. It is a vision that reminds us how all things worldly have a beginning, thus an end. The material universe is no different than human mortality.

When John was shown "the holy city, the new Jerusalem coming down out of heaven from God," that **new** state was like Jesus's **new** commandment to **his** disciples – **his** little children.

That change was not about all mortals getting a start-over, as a future time when all sins are forgiven. To think that is to fail to see the truth of everything Jesus preached.

The holy city that is the new Jerusalem came down out of heaven from God **WHENEVER** a new Apostle was born, **in the name of Jesus Christ**. The end of one's world as a sinner means a soul that no longer feels the limitations of a mortal body of flesh. The old world has passed away to a new way of being. Those souls seek the love of other such saved souls ... to love one another **in the name of Jesus Christ**.

We have to act as apostles in order to have our souls freed from this material realm. **THEN**, when God brings down the holy city to make the "home of God [be] among mortals," only those who will have proved their soul's ability to serve God and Christ will be there.

The souls that chose to hate Jesus Christ, the souls that chose to betray Jesus Christ, and the souls that chose to mingle with a secular world that was designed to trick little children into eating forbidden foods ... those souls will have passed with the first heaven and the first earth.

It was with the love between one another that God proclaimed, "I am the Alpha and the Omega, the beginning and the end. To the thirsty I will give water as a **gift** from the spring **of the water of life**."

God is always. God knows all. We are lost without God leading us from within.

So, we are not allowed to pretend to be a god, trying to save the planet, trying to welcome our enemies into our midst, and trying to determine what Jesus would do, if Jesus were still here.

As the saying goes, "You are what you eat," or better stated: "A man is what he eats." As far as souls are concerned, if you seek to be fed manna as spiritual nourishment and desire to be given the water of life to drink, then you will be one of the **new holy city** mortals.

If you find epicurean philosophy most fulfilling, seeking the pleasures provided by fleshy foods, with a thirst for knowledge and material wealth, then your soul will remain in the old earth's realm.

We cannot change the rules to suit our wants and desires. Jesus has been here – **on earth** – every day since his Ascension. On the Day of Pentecost Jesus returned.

That was when his Mind filled all of the "apostles and believers" for the first time. Jesus has been reborn in every apostle ever since then, showing how he has loved his disciples, showing them how to keep loving one another as he has loved them.

Jesus is Christ, the Son of God, the Alpha and the Omega. Each apostle has become a reborn Jesus ... in multitudes that cannot be counted. The names of the human forms that have walked as a new Jesus have had names beginning with every letter of the alphabet ... alpha to omega.

When the New Jerusalem comes, you do not want to realize then what Peter meant when he said, "Who was I that could hinder God?"

"Praise God, heaven of heavens, and you waters

above the heavens."

"He has raised up strength for his people and praise for all his loyal servants, the children of Israel, a people who are near him."

"Hallelujah!"

Amen

# SIXTH SUNDAY OF EASTER

# YEAR C

**Relevant readings:**
Acts 16:9-15
Psalm 67
Revelation 21:10 &
Revelation 21:22-27 &
Revelation 22:1-5
John 14:23-29 or
John 5:1-9

## Now is the time to start planning for which "retirement home" you want

[Happy Eastern Orthodox Easter!!!]

# Easter Sermons: Sixth Sunday of Easter, Year C

My mother was one of twelve children.

She was one of seven daughters and five sons, born to an Alabama sharecropper and his wife.

My mother remembered picking cotton in the fields on cold fall mornings before school, till her fingers were raw and chilled to the bone. As a small child, she said, she was not allowed to stop working until her "little shoe was full of cotton seeds."

My mother moved to the "big city" as soon as she turned seventeen. By then, World War II was underway and young American men were away fighting. That meant women could find work away from the farms.

I was raised in and around that big city. I was born into a time when that war was over and our men had returned to also seek work away from the farms.

My grandparents had twelve children because each child was an extra farmhand. The more children the parents had, the easier the workloads became. Still, life was hard and everyone had to lend a hand.

As a boy growing up, most of the families in my neighborhood had between one and three children.

I recall how television reflected this new American family size. While *The Waltons* showed a large, rural family, that was the exception to the new rule. That fictional family was set into a depression era, when (like my mother's family) the more hands around the more stability there was under one roof.

Robert Tippett

The family of the 1950's were reflected in *My Three Sons* (three sons, father and uncle), *Bonanza* (three sons, father only), *Father Knows Best* (son, two daughters, father and mother), *Leave It To Beaver* (two sons, father and mother), *The Addams Family* (one son, one daughter, father, mother, aunt and uncle), *The Munsters* (son, cousin, father, mother and grandfather), and (of course) *The Andy Griffith Show* (one son, father and aunt). All had families with one, two or three children ... although in some shows one son would leave the show and an adoptee or ranch hand would be added to the cast, to maintain the original numbers.

America had changed to smaller families, because work was easier for fathers to find in the big cities. In addition, city work paid more, so mothers could stay home and raise the kids.

Sometimes the mother had died, so an uncle would move in to help the father manage his children, or a grandparent would help out. When the father was land wealthy and the kids had grown to young men, the whole family used their position of wealth to help their neighbors.

While that is a Hollywood view of American family life, experiencing poverty and rationing was why my mother became a hoarder. I know others of her generation likewise found it hard to throw something potentially useful away.

They hoarded because they lived through all or part of the Great Depression and World War II. They knew the pains and hardships of poverty. They knew the values of things they had to do without.

# Easter Sermons: Sixth Sunday of Easter, Year C

They knew how **hard** life can be when you are a child of poor parents, in difficult times.

The transformation of American, from many children to few, was a statement about not enjoying growing up "lost in a crowd," where special attention was always hard to find. It was a statement about having children in numbers that suit your financial means ... so children never had to know the meaning of hard work.

My generation was the first of a pampered group of Americans. We are called the "Baby Boomers." We came from poor parents that had just enough to afford us higher education, to place us in cities that offered part-time jobs, so we could subsidize our "allowance" and learn the value of wages.

My generation grew to spawn "Generation X" and "Generation Y," who became the "Me Generations." We also taught our children the meaning of divorce, drug use acceptance, progressive secularism, and declining religious values. Chasing dollars has a way of making people forget what is most important ... family values.

Now, our children have given rise to "Millennials." They seem to have little knowledge of any work ethic, moral values, or meaningful educational skills. I watched my son spend hour upon hour playing video games; and now gaming and computer programming are the new industries. Nobody picks cotton or does manual labor, it seems.

And we wonder why the average age of Christian churches is getting older and older, with children dwindling in attendance. The reason is no longer smaller family sizes.

All of this history comes to us thanks to our parents or grandparents leaving the farm for the big cities. We left our roots behind, so we have forgotten how **hard work** is a vital part of our existence.

The saying is: "Spare the rod, spoil the child." Well, <u>life</u> is the rod that beats human beings to death. It always has been, and it always will be that way. When you spare the lesson of <u>life</u> from the child, everything falls apart.

This is the message today in the readings. It is a message that is most clear, but one that we are blinded from seeing.

Actually, there are two possible Gospel readings for today, and both bear the same message. In John 14 we read how Jesus told Judas (not Iscariot), "Those who love me will keep my teaching." And, "Whoever does not love me does not keep my words."

Jesus then made the **profound** statement: "I do not give to you as the world gives."

Without saying as much, but based on the "love" parameters established prior, that means, "If you love me, then you will give to others as I give to you, which is **not** as the world gives."

When you think about that lesson from John 14:23-29, you can then read the lesson from John 5:1-9, where Jesus saw a man "who had been ill for thirty-eight years." That man was at the pool by the Sheep Gate, in Jerusalem.

Jesus asked that man, "Do you want to be made well?"

# Easter Sermons: Sixth Sunday of Easter, Year C

The man heard that simple question like one made by a world that often uses words of encouragement, as if Jesus was asking the man, "What can I do to give you a hand?"

The ill man replied to Jesus, "Sir, I have no one to put me into the pool when the water is stirred up; and while I am making my way [dragging myself with my hands, slowly], someone else steps down ahead of me."

It was believed that the first person in the whirlpool would be cured of an ailment. So, the man never was the first one in the pool.

The man answered Jesus's question with, "Yes, give me a helping hand," instead of "Yes, sir. I do want to be made well."

Jesus gave to the man in a way that was **not** like the world gives. Jesus simply **gave** him his **words** that said, "Stand up, take you mat and walk."

Jesus gave the Holy Spirit to the man through **thought**, so "at once the man was made well."

That example means that Jesus told Judas (not Iscariot) to help people with **the word** of the Holy Spirit. Give them salvation through **faith**. If you try to play god and force everyone away from the edge of the pool, so your selected poor person can slink in first … probably not to be made well … then you prove you do not love Jesus.

In the reading from the Acts of the Apostles, we read how Paul had a vision in the night. He saw "a man of Macedonia pleading with him and saying, "Come over to Macedonia and help us."

Can you see how that vision of Paul's **has to be exactly how** Jesus saw the man "who had been ill for thirty-eight years"? Jesus was not as old as that man; but he **knew** the lame man had been lying there a long time.

Jesus had a <u>vision</u> of this man amid a crowd of sick people, but it was this man's **faith** that pleaded with Jesus, saying, "Come over here and help me."

Seeing and hearing such a vision is how one proves he or she is loving God and keeping his word. After thirty-eight years of failures, the lame man had not given up his belief in God's miracles.

When you understand that, imagine how the riders at this bus stop would approach some place in the world that is filled with crowds of ill, poor people, who sit and wait to be the first to be saved, only to be there a lifetime waiting.

Would you wait for a vision to come in the night, telling you specifically where God and Christ needed **you** to go? If the call in a vision says, "Come to that place," would you go?

Would **you** then immediately drop everything and go there to do God's work, if you had a vision?

Paul did not have a clue who he would find in Macedonia, but he and Silas made their way there and just hung out for a few days. Then, on the Sabbath, they went looking for a place they "supposed was a place of prayer."

# Easter Sermons: Sixth Sunday of Easter, Year C

Then they began preaching about the meaning of Scripture, and how it had prophesied the coming of the Messiah, who was fulfilled in Jesus of Nazareth. They knew that because Jesus had died, been resurrected, and passed on the Holy Spirit of Salvation to his followers.

A woman named Lydia, who was a worshiper of God, **heard the word of Jesus** ... the **love** of Jesus ... and not only she, but her whole household ... the women at that place Paul and Silas preached ... were <u>baptized</u>.

You have to understand that "<u>baptized</u>" means they were filled with the Holy Spirit.

Because Lydia was a woman of faith and because she had a household of women who worshipped God like she did, they were given a **spiritual gift** unlike any the world has to offer.

Raise your hand if you have given your love of Jesus Christ to a group of people in need, so that they were moved by the Holy Spirit.

<look for raised hands>

We do a lot of selfish things in the name of Christianity. We, in that case, are like all the invalids – the blind, the lame, and the paralyzed – waiting by the pool of healing for ourselves to find a miracle cure.

We inch closer and closer to heaven ... in our minds ... just like the lame would inch as close as possible to the whirlpool outside the Sheep Gate, ready to leap at the first sign

Robert Tippett

of personal benefit.

We wait silently ... because we dare not ever stop to talk to a fellow Christian about what the Holy Bible means. If we speak about our faith, someone might find out we aren't as Christian as we say we are, causing someone to make us move further away from that healing pool.

That is where it becomes **so** important to see how that whirlpool and the Sheep Gate are all part of the first Jerusalem, which we heard about last Sunday. The need for healing waters will pass away when the new city of Jerusalem comes down from heaven.

John wrote of that coming, saying "nothing unclean will enter it, nor anyone who practices abomination or falsehood, but only those who are written in the Lamb's book of life." That is like Jesus telling Judas (not Iscariot), "Whoever does not love me does not keep my words; and the word that you hear is not mine, but is from the Father who sent me."

If someone here today does not truly have God in his or her heart, and does not "keep the word" of Jesus always on their mind, through the Holy spirit's presence, then one truly does not love Jesus. Only those who **love** Jesus have their names "written in the Lamb's book of life."

Only those will be allowed in this new holy city of Jerusalem, because the first earth – where people left the farms to go to dirty, uncaring, "sell your souls for a dollar" cities and teach their children how to help themselves and not others – that earth will pass away, and with it will pass away the souls who did not have the name "Jesus" on their foreheads.

Think about that for just one moment.

<pause>

I have been preaching so often about this that I wonder if it is sinking in.

When John wrote, "the throne of God and of the Lamb will be in [the new holy city of Jerusalem], and [God's] servants will worship him; they will see his face, and [the Lamb's] name will be on their foreheads," this means that the only souls allowed into this new city will be those of the first earth who were reborn as Jesus.

That name has to be on one's forehead by the Mind of Christ leading one, just as Jesus was willingly led. That is why Jesus told Judas (not Iscariot), "The word that you hear [which is mine, which you will prove your **love** by keeping] is not [from my brain as] mine, but is from the Father who sent me."

Christ wore the name "Jesus" on the forehead of the human form that God inhabited, via the Holy Spirit. All apostles since have worn the same name – "Jesus" – because the same God has sent them the same Holy Spirit, for them to keep the same word.

This Easter season, as the resurrected Jesus sits with us today – external to our bodies and souls – not having his name yet written on us disciples' foreheads – we are learning valuable lessons about who we will serve when the day of Pentecost comes.

We need to be planning ahead **<u>now</u>**!

Will we be one of those who sacrificed some worldly gifts for an eternity of bliss in the new heaven and the new earth, where "nothing accursed will be found there anymore"?

Or will we marked as not clean and outcast?

Can you see **yourself** in that vision Paul had? Can you see **your soul** as pleading with an apostle of Christ and saying, "Come over to **me** and help **me**!"?

Can you see yourself as one who believes in miracles – the river of the water of life – but although your brain is willing, your flesh is week?

Do you sit crippled and lame near healing water, hoping someone will come **give** you eternal life?

"Stand up, take you mat and **walk**."

Walk to wherever God sends you a vision to go; but know when you get there, then **you** have to preach <u>the word of the Lord</u> … out of **love**.

"The earth has brought forth her increase; may God, our own God, <u>give</u> us his blessing."

Amen

# SEVENTH SUNDAY OF EASTER

# YEAR C

**Relevant readings:**
Acts 16:16-34
Psalm 97
Revelation 22:12-21
John 17:20-26

## See! I am coming sooner than you might think

Last week, I whispered before the sermon, "Happy Eastern Orthodox Easter!" Today, we are at the seventh Sunday of Easter, according to the Roman Catholic calculations. Thus, we celebrated Easter seven weeks ago, on March 27th. The Eastern Church is connected to the Jewish

# Easter Sermons: Seventh Sunday of Easter, Year C

Passover, such that their Easter is 35 days after ours ... this year ... five Sundays after - five weeks.

Next Sunday **we** will celebrate the Day of Pentecost. Since the Greek word *"pentékosté"* means "fiftieth," the capitalized version (*"Pentēkostēs"*) along with the word "day" (*"hēmeran"*) means the special day the Jews celebrated. However, if you do the math ... seven weeks of seven days means today is the 49th day ...

So, tomorrow should be the Fiftieth Day ... the Day of Pentecost ...

But it is not, as next Sunday ... the 56th day is ... I assume because it is recognized on the closest Sunday after the seventh Sunday?

It is confusing, but Christians in the West begin a count on the Saturday before Easter Sunday, so today is like the forty-third day, making next Sunday the fiftieth day.

I think?

Still, the Eastern Orthodox Church will recognize the Day of Pentecost on Sunday, June 19th ... but the Jews will recognize *Shavuot* between June 11-13, where the Fiftieth Day is June 11, a Saturday [*Shabbat*] and Sunday being June 12.

The Jews begin the "counting of the omer" on the second day of the Passover Festival (eight days long); but both the Eastern and Western churches begin their counts on Easter Sunday ... after the Passover festival ended on a *Shabbat*.

So, if you are confused, it is okay. It seems everyone is.

The main point of any Easter "counting" is we Christians should be learning how to believe Jesus is the Christ ... knowing full well that Jesus was prophesied all throughout the Old Testament, perfectly fulfilling that in what we read in the Gospels. The counting is then setting an expectation for when Christ fills us with the Holy Spirit and we can begin our individual ministries.

The **long** season that follows Pentecost – called Ordinary Time - is named that because we are <u>ordained</u> by the Holy Spirit. Ordinary time is then when **we** are called to spread **<u>the word</u>** of Jesus, so others can also be filled with the Holy Spirit.

So, be prepared. Next week summer school begins ... for those who don't make the grade as ordained priests this year.

Today is like the final exam for the 2016 graduating class.

<pause>

Please don't be dismayed if you just now realized how little you have prepared for your **personal** ordination as a priest for the One God ... becoming a **<u>true</u>** Christian ... because one of the marvels of the Easter lessons is they show us that there is still a chance to instantly be filled with the Holy Spirit.

Cornelius was a Gentile, as were his Roman soldiers; and they <u>suddenly</u> became baptized in the Holy Spirit.

Lydia was a Gentile, as were the women of her household

who were praying by the river; and they all were <u>instantly</u> filled with the Holy Spirit.

Today, we learn how a Philippian jailer "and his entire family were baptized <u>without delay</u>."

All of those were **baptized** ... by the Holy Spirit .. not by water.

There were no tests to be passed then ... sort of.

Even Tabitha, who was a good disciple, who believed in Jesus as the Christ, she died without having been filled with the Holy Spirit. But, when Peter came and prayed over her corpse and then stood and spoke from the Holy Spirit's voice, "Tabitha, get up," she was <u>immediately</u> filled with those waters of life. She was resurrected by the Holy Spirit.

The key here, in all these stories of **<u>sudden</u>** comings of the Holy Spirit, is the Spirit came upon those who lived good, God-fearing lives, and who often prayed to God for guidance ... as Gentiles <u>of faith</u>.

**Still** ... in addition to that most basic requirement, faith and works of faith are **not enough** ... they listened to <u>the word</u> that was spoken by an apostle **AND** then their hearts were opened to receive that **word**.

That was all they had to do to "pass their graduation exams."

They were not asked to choose correctly from multiple choice questions about Bible studies they had never attended. No fill-in-the-blank names were asked to be identified, to prove they came to church each Sunday and listened to the readings. None had to write essays about the meaning of Easter or how to count the omer, to determine when Pentecost should be.

They just had to be God-fearing and Jesus-believing, while praying not to be lost in a world of sin ... **AND** ... they had to hear the **word** spoken by an apostle.

Listen now.

<pause>

In the reading from John's *Revelation*, we find Jesus's voice – **<u>his Word</u>** – saying, "See, I am coming soon."

Open your hearts and hear that message.

<pause>

It is **not** a message about some distant time ... as a time representative of the end of this sinful world, which has been prophesied to be the fate of <u>others</u> ... fortunately not you.

<u>WRONG ANSWER</u> if you thought that!

"See, I am coming soon" is about **YOU** and **NOW**! It always means that ... to those who can <u>hear</u> Jesus talking the **Word** at all times.

The Greek John wrote actually says, "Experience ... I come speedily," although that can be stated as "See, I am coming soon."

It means, however, Jesus comes <u>instantly</u> …<u>quickly</u> … <u>immediately</u> … to those whose lives have been doing good works, showing love to others, and praying to God for guidance and help.

You just have to be like Cornelius, Tabitha, Lydia, and the Philippian jailer and **hear the word**, so it speaks to you **in your heart**.

Jesus said to John, "My reward is with me." That means the value of believing in Jesus as the Christ is only seen when **you** are **<u>with</u>** Christ. Together ... and **only** together ... is the reward of Christ found.

John then said Jesus would return **soon**, "to repay according to everyone's work." That included Gentiles who did good deeds … unselfish works … and acts of loving kindness towards others. The reward of Christ **only** comes from proper actions ... never to reward inaction.

In a way, Jesus is coming <u>quickly</u> at the end of **your** world ... which is when you die of ego-driven self and become a devoted servant of God. Tabitha died in her material body and was resurrected. The jailer died figurative, by drawing his sword to end his life ... but he was resurrected by the **<u>word</u>** spoken through Paul: "Do not harm yourself, for we are all here."

"Jailer, get up." was the essence of that command.

When Jesus said, "I am the Alpha and the Omega, the first and the last, the beginning and the end," it means

God's Messiah has been **"with"** all of God's holy servants, throughout **all** time.

**Every** apostle of Christ has been one with Christ, with that union between "the Spirit and the bride." That means a resurrected Jesus in the one receiving the Spirit. They all had to die of self and be reborn as Jesus.

It is precisely as Jesus prayed for his disciples – of which <u>YOU</u> claim to be one – "The glory that [God the Father has] given to me I give to **you**, so that **you** may be one, as we are one."

Jesus then prayed, "Righteous Father, the world does not know you … [but] I will make [God the Father] known, so that the **love** with which you have loved me may be **in them, <u>and I in them</u>**."

In the *Revelation*, we are told how we **<u>must</u>** pray, "Come, Lord Jesus!"

In return, "The grace of the Lord Jesus be with all the saints."

Easter Sermons: Seventh Sunday of Easter, Year C

Sinners are not "saints." Disciples are not "saints" **Only** apostles filled with the Holy Spirit become holy and righteous enough to be deemed "saints."

Therefore, "Blessed are those who wash their [priestly – as are disciples'] robes, so that they will have the right to the tree of life."

You **must** graduate from being a sinful robed wannabe Christian – still a Gentile plebe – to becoming a **SAINT**.

Alone no one is saintly. **Only** when **with** Christ, God, and the Holy Spirit can that happen.

The end of the first heaven and the first earth will bring about the new holy city of Jerusalem, which will be without a temple. That absence will be because all mortals will become the temples to God. Their robes will have been washed clean by the blood of the Lamb, as **only** saints can be temples for the Lord.

No sinners will be allowed there, then. God will not be playing horseshoes then, where close counts. Not even "leaners" will be counted.

In this Easter season, as with all Easter seasons, it is <u>school time with Jesus</u>. You must learn to receive the Holy Spirit to graduate from that school.

Some see "the Day of Pentecost" as some official day when the Holy Spirit overcomes one, as if only one day a year is that miracle allowed to happen.

Others, such as the group of Christians who believe speaking in tongues can be taught to believers, those who call themselves Pentecostals, there is no such limitation.

They see speaking in tongues as a mandatory tenet. Many members display that "talent" openly, during church services ... year round. They stand and make babbling noises with their mouths. The other members respect that ability as a way of praising God.

However, Pentecost means "Fiftieth Day." It is when Moses returned from the mount with the Commandments, so that the Law of God was **with** the Israelites. Therefore, when the disciples morphed into apostles on the Fiftieth Day, that transformation showed how Jesus Christ was **with** each of them ... suddenly and immediately ... because the Law of God had become a personal, faithful love in their hearts.

This fast, but without damage or pain.

The whole family of Jesus was filled with the Holy Spirit ... disciples and their relatives who followed and supported Jesus's ministry ... just as we read during the Easter Season how the households and families of Cornelius, Lydia and the Philippian jailer were so **baptized**.

Baptized with the Holy Spirit ... not with water.

Those households became the earliest churches of Christ, meaning **ALL** members of those churches were filled with the Holy Spirit. That means it is a mandatory step towards becoming a **true** Christian.

Let me tell you a story from my younger days, when I was

raised in an Assemblies of God church ... a Pentecostal church. I have not told it in some time, but bear with me if you have heard it before.

The cathedral I was raised in had a room designated for prayer – a prayer room. In it members would pray, as well as teach other members to speak in tongues. That process meant kneeling at a folding chair, eyes closed, hands raised high in the air, while repeating the word "glory" over and over and over.

That repetition, done faster and faster, eventually made one's tongue get tied up so that one started making noises, rather than saying "glory."

One weekday evening (either a Tuesday or Friday), a travelling evangelist came to our church to preach and at the end's altar call he asked for volunteers to come and speak in tongues. Me and my friend the same age (about thirteen) – neither having spoken in tongues before – stepped forward as volunteers.

My friend and I were doing the standard "glory" thing on the altar steps, with all the attending congregation surrounding us two, while the travelling evangelist (mic in hand still) kept the excitement level high. Then the evangelist leaned over and whispered in my ear, "Say whatever comes into your mind."

Immediately, I began making babbling noises. He suggested and I responded. The travelling evangelist praised the Lord, as did all the congregation ... including my mother ... because I had spoken in tongues.

I knew I had said nothing of value; but for a while, I felt proud that I had pleased so many people. I began to tell myself, "This is easy," and I would recreate the babbling as I walked privately … like praying … as if I had become special.

Then I realized I had been tricked.

That is, until many years later, when I realized the travelling evangelist had spoken the truth about how fast the Holy Spirit comes upon one of God's faithful. Speaking in divine languages (understanding Scripture) does cause one to "say whatever comes into one's mind" … but God does not make human beings babble like idiots or say wrong things.

Babbling like an idiot in the name of the Lord is no different than thinking some water sprinkled on one's head will make one a **SAINT**. Both are acts of misguided faith, because Scripture tells us so.

The Holy Spirit, sent by Christ to the faithful, makes Christians **hear** so they can **preach** the **word of truth**. That is so other ears can hear and be affected. It takes years of wanting to serve God and Christ, and years of prayer, and years of repentance, with years of good works. However, once one is prepared to serve, the Lord will come quickly.

The Holy Spirit comes quickly to those who hear the word in their hearts. The selfish have seals around that vital organ, preventing it from opening up to God and Christ. God does not come privately to human beings, so they can ignore others and gossip, snicker, and ridicule those who faithfully follow false concepts.

# Easter Sermons: Seventh Sunday of Easter, Year C

God does not choose people to be special. God chooses special people to be his priests ... His willing servants.

It requires faith to misunderstand when Easter is, or when the Day of Pentecost is. It requires faith to think speaking in tongues is just as easy as standing before a crowd and making noises with your mouth. It requires faith to hear, "John baptizes you with water, but Jesus will baptize you with the Holy Spirit," and think, "I am saved because I was christened as a baby."

The Acts of the Apostles is a book telling about the ordination of priests for the One God, where the first step taken by all was **faith**. An ordination by the Holy Spirit follows belief, which is demonstrated through good deeds. Filled with the Holy Spirit means one gladly and joyfully accepts a **lifetime** of service to God and Christ ... doing good works, based on the talents given by the Holy Spirit.

In order to receive that task of labor, you **must** see, feel, and know that doing **nothing** - now - is selfish; and as such, do-nothings will be rewarded "according to those works" ... meaning nothing holy will come to them.

Excuses are like pieces of lumber used to build a funeral pyre. The work do-nothings do ... avoiding good works for others ... is not God-fearing. It is evil fearing.

Thus David sang:

> "The Lord loves those who hate evil; he preserves the lives of his saints and delivers them from the hands of the wicked."

"Light has sprung up for the righteous, and joyful gladness for those who are true-hearted."

"Rejoice in the Lord, you righteous, and give thanks to his holy Name."

Amen

# Easter Sermons: Seventh Sunday of Easter, Year C

# PENTECOST SUNDAY

# YEAR C

**Relevant readings:**
Acts 2:1-21 or
Genesis 11:1-9
Psalm 104:25-37
Romans 8:14-17 or
Acts 2:1-21
John 14:8-17 and
John 14:25-27

## Hearing about God's deeds of power

My mother worked at Sears when I was growing up. It seems that everything we owned came from Sears.

# Easter Sermons: Pentecost Sunday, Year C

Many things my mother would bring home had "Some Assembly Required." As the "man of the house," I got to put it all together.

I learned three things from that history:

> 1. Follow the instructions;
> 2. Have the right tools; and
> 3. Have a can or jar ready for spare parts or pieces you forgot to put on when you are finished.

As I got older and began driving, I learned it was less costly to do my own basic auto maintenance – brakes, oil changes, filter changes, tire pressure checks, etc. It was less expensive paying for parts at an Autozone, than it was to take the car to an auto mechanic's shop.

Following my experience of putting things together, I would regularly buy a shop manual for each car I owned. It is rule number one to have a set of instructions for doing one's own car maintenance.

Additionally, following rule two, I would buy gadgets like an oil filter wrench, a long plastic funnel, a spark plug socket for my ratchet set, an oil-can-piercing spout and a plastic pan for draining oil. In essence, I made my garage my auto maintenance shop.

In those younger years when I did my own automotive work, I found it was best to plan about five hours of my time to do what a real mechanic could get done in 30 minutes. This is because I found out that my actual cars never exactly matched the pictures of similar cars that were found in the shop manual. This meant I needed extra time so I could do considerable head scratching. That was in addition to the standard time for medical attention I needed, from scraping my knuckles, elbows, and knees. The pain and suffering is a natural add-on cost that comes from doing things that others are far more capable of doing.

I found out there was a lot of trial and error in my work. I always ended up redoing something done wrong (often more than once), as well as making trips back to the auto parts store because I bought the wrong part.

I learned over the years, from experience, that futility was part of my "fix-it karma." I never seemed to be on the same page as those who wrote the 'fix-it' books I bought.

Many times ... usually after something had been taken apart and seemed like it would never be put back together properly by me ... I would have a conversation with God. Often I asked him, "Why me? Why do I try to do these things?"

Usually, that talk would calm me and allow me to wipe the blood, sweat, and tears away, take a deep breath and then try one more time. Amazingly, a miracle of temporary genius would overcome me and allow me to see my way out the corners I would paint myself into, so the work would be finished.

After all the sweat and grime had been washed away and a cooler head reappeared, I would realize that it was my inability to read the shop manual, or it was my going through the instructions too quickly that led to all of my problems. I suffered from "user error," which comes from not regularly putting things together for a living.

# Easter Sermons: Pentecost Sunday, Year C

The readings for this first Sunday that puts us on the cusp of Ordinary Time brings recognition of how the disciples turned into apostles on the Jewish day of Pentecost. All the readings focus on failures to understand the language of God ... misreading the instructions, so to speak.

The Holy Bible is a collection of books written in a way that requires one to be knowledgeable of God's specific terminology that He speaks to His priests. In that same specificity, a set of shop manuals are written in a language that is readily understood by trained mechanics, but not novices like myself and many others.

Thus, I make the comparison of "Speaking in Tongues" to "Some Assembly Required." As easy as it is for a layperson to think, "How hard can it be?" the reality is it will always be as difficult as you make it.

Whether it is the Gospel of John, or *Chilton's 1988 Honda Accord Shop Manual*, or a set of instructions for an IKEA futon, you have to speak the language that is spoken ... **fluently** ... if your expectations of accomplishment from understanding are going to be met.

Even though the original Hebrew and Greek texts of the books of the Holy Bible have been translated into English – for us English-speaking Americans to understand – those translations are varied. One word's translation one place can often mean another word in used translation elsewhere.

This is like the Genesis story of the Tower of Babel, when God divided the languages of the world. From mortals having only one language to understand, a potential for danger was seen. This danger is because God knows not everyone can equally master instructions, tools, and control excess and waste. Therefore, God confused mankind's ability to understand, so mankind would have to work harder and learn from its mistakes ... by divine design.

The Tower of Babel becomes a reflection of a "**word**" problem. Two points of focus are easily seen: earth and heaven. The problem is getting to heaven from earth. The simple solution to make that transition is build a tower. However, God made sure nothing is ever that simple.

Solving a word problem is more than seeing one answer. It requires being able to see what further problems will come from one solution to a past problem. Mankind struggles seeing into the future and solving problems, when it will has struggled in certain areas in the past. This is why mankind **needs** God and should not have an immediate ability to understand one language without God.

The language confusion set in place by God is then how all of the Holy Bible is written. An example is read today when Jesus told his disciples, "I go and prepare a place for you [at my Father's house], [and] I will come back and take you to be with me that you also may be where I am. You know the way to the place where I am going."

Confusion is why Thomas would say, "Lord, we don't know where you are going, so how can we know the way?"

To Thomas, what Jesus had said was like me reading, "Take a 3/8" washer and apply to one 1 ¼" screw inserted through part 419, secured with one "Y" lock nut"

# Easter Sermons: Pentecost Sunday, Year C

If not knowing where Jesus's Father's house is located was difficult for the disciples to comprehend – and they had consumed a number of cups of wine at the Seder meal so they were not clearheaded – it is easy to see how confused they were when Jesus then said:

> "Believe me that I am in the Father and the Father is in me; but if you do not, then believe me because of the works themselves. Very truly, I tell you, the one who believes in me will also do the works that I do and, in fact, will do greater works than these, because I am going to the Father."

As Christians today, roughly two thousand years removed from that evening's conversation in Jerusalem, we think we understand what that means. However, that is only the Big Brain Syndrome making us think that.

It is like standing at the auto parts store thumbing through a shop manual for a 1988 Honda Accord and thinking, "I can do this."

It is no different than Philip asking Jesus, "Lord, show us the Father, and we will be satisfied."

That is no different than him saying, "Give us a manual, Lord, and we will all be fine."

In this ultra-modern computer world we don't think we have the time to learn everything about everything, so we just want to go to Google Maps and print out the directions to the Father's house – step by step, with distances to gauge each step by. [Now it is GPS on smart phones.]

The dividing of the languages was so someone – anyone – who is not prepared to understand **will not understand**. Understanding is dangerous … if one is not prepared by God first.

In the reading from the Acts of the Apostles, a major part of the focus is placed on remembering how the Holy Spirit suddenly came upon the disciples. We read it was "like the rush of a violent wind." Some get shivers imagining how the disciples were given "divided tongues, as of fire," which appeared instantly.

Then the new apostles began speaking fluently in foreign languages … languages they had never been trained to know.

It was as miraculous as if I suddenly was able to put together an IKEA futon without needing to glance at the instructions, using only the "universal wrench" included in the parts bag, so I could tighten all the nuts and screws.

What is almost completely overlooked in the Acts story is how eleven "Babblers" were able to stop a large crowd of pilgrims, causing them to remark, "Are not all these who are speaking Galileans? And how is it we hear, each of us, in our own native language … them **speaking about God's deeds of power**?"

The words the new apostles spoke were reaching all of those pilgrims and causing "Aha moments".

It was like suddenly realizing that the difference between a "A" screw and a "B" screw can be determined by placing a physical screw up to the scaled pictures of screws, printed on the instructions. It was like being handed some step-by-step directions to the Father's house.

All of those pilgrim Jews – in Jerusalem for the commanded festival of *Shavuot* [Weeks] – had not only read the Scriptures but they had discussed them every *Shabbat*. They recognized God's words, but not in the way the apostles were then explaining them.

**Suddenly** – a bunch of hillbilly Galileans were telling those devoted pilgrims the true depth of meaning that was contained ... hidden in those Hebrew words. The apostles were fluently speaking **meaning**, when nary a one of them had ever been to prophet school and graduated as an official scribe for Herod's Temple.

All at once, all of the Jews received the talent of divided tongues, and they could fluently speak the languages of those who had been scattered around the known world. They suddenly understood "one language and the same words." (Genesis 11:1)

One mind had been joined with them all - the Mind of Christ's understanding of the one language of God.

This communication via the spoken/written language "is the Spirit of truth, whom the world cannot receive, because it neither sees him nor knows him." A world of divided tongues can only come together under one common language when it knows God through the Holy Spirit.

Knowing God through the Holy Spirit requires the instruction manual be read first ... especially the part that says, "If you love me, you will keep my commandments."

Also important is: "Believe Jesus that Jesus is in the Father and the Father is in Jesus."

"Believe in Jesus so you too can do the works that Jesus did," which includes understanding the one language of God.

Now, when the shock and awe of the apostles "speaking of God's deeds of power" wore off a little, some of the devoted Jews who heard that truth sneered.

They did that because that truth the apostles spoke had never been heard before. That caused them to say, "They are filled with new wine."

That also was the truth ... only not in a literal sense. Peter denied they had been drinking fermented grape juice early in the morning.

The apostles (**AND** soon three thousand Jewish listening pilgrims) were filled with the "new wine" of the Holy Spirit. This was a fulfillment of what would later be written, about a past event:

> "[Jesus] gave [the cup] to them, saying, "Drink from it, all of you. This is my blood of the covenant, which is poured out for many for the forgiveness of sins. I tell you, I will not drink from this fruit of the vine from now on <u>until that day when I drink it **new** with you in my Father's kingdom</u>." (Matthew 26:27-29)

Jesus was back on the day of Pentecost, multiplied twelve

times, returning **as them** as they drank the "blood of Jesus" - the Holy Spirit.

To explain this in terms that had already been written and known by devout Jews, Peter quoted from the prophet Joel, saying:

> "In the last days it will be, God declares,
>
> that I will pour out my Spirit upon all flesh,
>
> and your sons and your daughters shall prophesy,
>
> and your young men shall see visions,
>
> and your old men shall dream dreams." (Joel 2:28)

All of those Jews then linked to the one common language of God, through the Holy Spirit. They had read those prophetic words many times before and **thought** they referred to the end of the world. They thought the "last days" would be much later than **that** day of Pentecost.

Yet, Peter quoted that prophecy as being fulfilled **then**, in their presence, with them being part of that fulfillment.

The actual Hebrew ("*wə-hā-yāh 'a-ḥă-rê- kên*") says, "Will come to pass after this," where "**this**" is a one-word-statement of what follows textually (the pouring out of God's Spirit). In the Greek text of John, Peter is said to have stated from Joel, "*estai en tais eschatais hēmerais*," which translates as, "will be in the end days."

Since both introductory statements lead to God pouring out

his Holy Spirit, into sons, daughters, old and young, the "after this" and the "end days" means the "final hours" of one's ignorance to God.

It is the end of having divided tongues and confusion. It is the **now** of whenever that Spirit is received by one of faith.

It is the beginning of being the fulfillment of, "You know [the Father], because he abides with you, and he will be in you."

It is the truth behind Paul's words to the Christians of Rome:

> "All who are led by the Spirit of God are children of God."

A true "child of God" is not a Jew. It is one who is reborn as Jesus ... **with God** in one's heart, **knowing God** through the Mind of Christ, and **becoming righteous** as Jesus. A Saint is the rebirth of a priest in the order of Melchizedek.

With the Holy Spirit as your being, uplifting your soul to the Lord, "you have received a spirit of adoption."

That is how **all** true Christians call out, "*Abba!* Father!"

That cry is not because we honor God with the title of Father, as the maker of all Creation. We call out "Father!" because we have become His Son or Daughter, through adoption; and whether we are young or old.

The path to the room reserved for us at the Father's house is where you sit on the bus stop bench right **now**. The path to God is within each of us ... via our souls.

Today we, us who have heard the word and understand, are called to go forth and preach that word to all who will receive it. We speak in one tongue that only those with the ears of the Lord can hear.

We prophesy by explaining the sacred texts ... God's deeds of power.

We go to where our visions call us to go.

We know what to expect to come, because we are led by our dreams that are poured out by the Holy Spirit.

We free those who are "slaves, both men and women," who have eyes to read but cannot see the truth.

We will go and teach them the common language of God, spoken through the Holy Spirit, so they too "shall prophesy" the word of God to others

That is the true meaning of the Fiftieth day. Pentecost is now about having the Spirit of God pour into one's flesh, fulfilling the prophecy of Joel and returning the faithful to understanding the one language of God.

Pentecost is the commanded Festival of Weeks, representing when the first fruits have matured and are fully consecrated as the children of God.

> "O Lord, how manifold are your works! In wisdom you have made them all."

Robert Tippett

"I will sing to the Lord as long as I live; I will praise my God while I have my being."

"May these words of mine please him; I will rejoice in the Lord."

Amen

# Easter Sermons: Pentecost Sunday, Year C

www.ingramcontent.com/pod-product-compliance
Lightning Source LLC
Chambersburg PA
CBHW030146100526
44592CB00009B/138